Finger Foods &
Party Snacks

Finger Food & Party Snacks

Over 75 recipes for fantastic party food

Consultant Editor
Linda Fraser

Acropolis
Books

First published by Lorenz Books in 1995

© Anness Publishing Limited 1995

Lorenz Books is an imprint of
Anness Publishing Limited
Boundary Row Studios
1 Boundary Row
London SE1 8HP

Distributed in Australia by Reed Editions

This edition distributed in Canada by Book Express
an imprint of Raincoast Books Distribution Limited.

ISBN 1 85967 074 1

A CIP catalogue record for this book
is available from the British Library

Editorial Director: Joanna Lorenz
Project Editor: Linda Fraser
Designers: Tony Paine and Roy Prescott
Photographers: Steve Baxter, Karl Adamson and Amanda Heywood
Food for Photography: Wendy Lee, Jane Stevenson and Elizabeth Wolf Cohen
Props Stylists: Blake Minton and Kirsty Rawlings
Additional recipes: Norma MacMillan, Carla Capalbo and Laura Washburn
Introductory text: Bridget Jones

ACKNOWLEDGEMENTS
For their assistance in the publication of this book
the publishers wish to thank:

Kenwood Appliances plc
New Lane
Havant
Hants
P09 2NH

Magimix
115A High Street
Godalming, Surrey
GU7 1AQ

Prestige
Prestige House
22–26 High Street
Egham,
Surrey
TW20 9DU

Le Creuset
The Kitchenware Merchants Ltd
4 Stephenson Close
East Portway
Andover
Hampshire
SP10 3RU

Printed and bound in Singapore

MEASUREMENTS
Three sets of equivalent measurements have been provided in the recipes here, in the following order:
Metric, Imperial and American. Do not mix units of measurement within each recipe.

 The apple symbol indicates a low fat, low cholesterol recipe.

CONTENTS

Introduction *6*

Dips, Nibbles and Pâtés *10*

Hot Finger Food *28*

Pizzas and Pastries *50*

Snacks and Sandwiches *66*

Simple Salads *84*

Index *96*

PERFECT PLANNING

Planning is the cornerstone for success on every occasion, from the grandest of celebrations to the simplest of impromptu parties with friends. Whatever the occasion, it is most important to have a clear outline of the form of entertaining before beginning to work on any of the preparations. A decision on the type and size of celebration is the starting point and the usual pre-arranging has to follow. Begin by considering your likely budget, then clearly outline what sort of party you are planning within the financial restrictions. Work through the following points, and by the time you have made notes on these you will have a structure for planning all the details.

TIME OF DAY

Is the event going to be cocktails or drinks before dinner, early supper, late supper, or drinks after dinner? If the party is linked to some outside event, check the exact timing for that.

FORMAL OR INFORMAL

The important thing is to decide exactly how you want to entertain, let everyone know what to expect and stick to your decision by planning accordingly. Think in terms of dress, how you expect guests to participate and the type of refreshments, and pass all this information on to the guests.

The type of entertainment and refreshment must fit in with the level of party – delicate canapés or hors d'oeuvre are perfect for cocktails, but not when guests are dressed for a walk in the park followed by a hearty brunch; and coping with unsuitable food or boisterous indoor games is awkward when standing and chatting in evening dress. Formal invitations will always state whether morning dress, evening dress or black tie (evening dress) are required. Informal dress, on the other hand, invariably demands some qualification because it can mean different things to different people. The best way to deal with this is to let guests know what sort of clothes you intend wearing – and not to change your mind later!

THE GUESTS

Bringing people together for small parties is not always easy and deciding on the group of people to invite to larger gatherings can be difficult. Nevertheless, this is an essential and important first step in good planning. If you organize a party for people who are strangers to one another, it is important to mix individuals who are likely to get on well together.

NUMBERS AND LOCATION

It is vital to make sure that you can cope with the numbers for the type of party planned. This is largely a matter of space, it is not practical to arrange a party for twenty-five in a house which is overfilled when half-a-dozen people are invited!

Remember that the equation can work the other way and that for some types of gatherings, success depends on having the party area fairly tightly packed with people – too few people in too large a space is fatal to creating any kind of party atmosphere. Decide whether your party is to take place indoors or outdoors, and whether you have sufficient space on home ground or should consider holding it elsewhere. For indoor entertaining at home, the main considerations are the room arrangements. Similarly, for outdoor events such as barbecues and parties in the garden on a modest scale, take a practical overview of patio space. Consider likely seating for those who require it, areas for children, the alternatives should the weather let the party down and so on.

FOOD AND DRINK

Whether the gathering is small or large, it is important to decide on the refreshments – snacks, finger food or some form of buffet – and to make sure the food and drink are suited to the occasion. This must be considered alongside the time of day, numbers invited, budget and location, where appropriate. You can be quite individual in your choice of refreshments as long as they fulfil the requirements for the time of day and location and adapt well to the style of party.

The level of refreshment offered must also correspond to the expected length of the party. Light canapés or hors d'oeuvre may be served for a late morning or mid-day affair when guests are expected to depart fairly quickly, but if you anticipate entertaining for the whole of the afternoon, the range of canapés or hors d'oeuvre must be extensive and plentiful or more substantial refreshment should be offered.

PARTY PREPARATIONS

This is the real business of party-giving, with fun being the key objective. How much food you make is up to you, but there should be sufficient refreshments to balance the alcohol intake. Either provide canapés, hors d'oeuvre and delicious nibbles for drinks parties and cocktail parties or make a large potful of something wholesome and serve it with a great bowl of rice or a stack of baked potatoes. Since most guests will find themselves a seat on the floor if the atmosphere is informal enough, presenting food which has to be eaten with the assistance of a knife is rarely a problem. Bread, cheese and pâté are all quick, easy and satisfying and don't dismiss platters of sandwiches with different tasty fillings which can be reserved for later in the evening.

Here are some suggestions and ideas to make your party a success:

◆ Clear the floor in one room to allow space for dancing. Set chairs aside but make sure that there are some comfortable areas where less lively guests can congregate and talk.

◆ The bar may be set up in the kitchen or towards one end of a large room. If you are entertaining a large number and have two rooms or a very spacious area, then it can be a good idea to have two bars. Do not use too small a table as there is a danger of glasses getting knocked off. Have a thick cloth on the table and pile plenty of clean towels and rolls of kitchen paper near. Place waste bags under the table.

◆ Order ice in advance from a local wine merchant or buy it from a convenience store. Buy drinks.

◆ Always have plenty of alcohol-free drinks: mineral water, soda water, lemonade, tonic, fruit juices, alcohol-free beer and low-alcohol wine.

◆ Make colourful ice cubes for mixed drinks and cocktails by freezing cherries, green olives, pieces of orange or lemon in water in ice cube trays.

◆ If you are short of chilling space, particularly for beers, then use a clean dustbin and tip a couple of large bags of ice into it. Pour in a couple of buckets of cold water. Stand this conveniently outside the back door and place all the unopened bottles and cans in it. Knot a few towels on the dustbin handles for wiping off chilled bottles and cans.

◆ Open-freeze orange and lemon slices by spreading them out on baking sheets lined with cling film. Adding lots of frozen fruit to punch helps to chill the drink. Frozen strawberries are colourful and they add flavour to a wine punch.

PARTY STYLE

A buffet is practical for large gatherings, such as weddings and formal parties. The buffet may consist of hot or cold dishes, or a combination of the two. Canapés or hors d'oeuvre may be served beforehand. Ideally, the buffet should consist of a choice of fish, poultry and meat dishes accompanied by a range of salads and vegetables.

It is usual to serve one course, just the main course at a buffet, followed by dessert and perhaps cheese.

Generally, these are larger events where the food offered is less central to the proceedings, although a formal buffet served for a wedding breakfast, for instance, involves the full panoply of a well-balanced meal. For most party events, offer a good range of nibbles and finger foods.

The food at cocktail parties is intended to whet the appetite rather than satisfy it – guests are intended to go on to a main meal elsewhere – although another school of thought decrees that cocktail snacks should be substantial to counteract the inebriating effects of the cocktails themselves. Canapés or hors d'oeuvre, nibbles and dips are the usual refreshments. They should be served in bite-sized portions and all be easy to eat with the fingers while balancing a glass at the same time. Any messy foods should be served on cocktail sticks.

COCKTAIL STYLE

The focal point of a cocktail party is the bar. Although the kitchen is an ideal location for this, it is more fun to locate your bar in the main reception room. Here are a few pointers to bear in mind when hosting a cocktail party.

◆ Make sure you have several cocktail shakers. Have a large jug and tall mixing stick for making thirst-quenching cocktails.

◆ Lay out different shapes and sizes of glasses on separate trays ready for different strengths of mixes. Offer mineral water, fruit juices and non-alcoholic alternatives on a separate table.

◆ Place large bowls of nibbles around the room, and make sure there are lots of canapés and finger food.

CLASSIC COCKTAILS

Bloody Mary Mix 1 measure vodka, a dash of Worcestershire sauce, a good squeeze lemon juice, 2 measures tomato juice and add seasoning to taste.

Buck's Fizz Orange juice topped up with champagne (or, for economy, dry sparkling wine) – about 1 part orange juice to 2 parts champagne.

Gin Sling Mix 2 measures gin, 1 measure cherry brandy, a squeeze of lemon juice, a twist of lemon rind and soda to top up.

Margarita Mix 3 measures tequila to 1 measure Cointreau. Frost the rim of the glass with lime juice and salt before pouring in the cocktail.

Martini Mix 1 measure gin to 1 measure dry vermouth. For a dry martini, mix 2 measures gin to 1 measure vermouth.

Piña Colada Equal measures of rum, pineapple juice and coconut milk, mixed in an electric blender and served on ice.

Pink Gin Gin with a dash of Angostura Bitters and topped with tonic water to taste.

DIFFERENT DRINK IDEAS

Apple and Brandy Top up brandy with unsweetened apple juice to taste. Serve with ice and a slice of lime.

Citrus Gin Mix 2 measures gin, 2 measures orange juice, 1 measure grapefruit.

Dairy Maid's Delight Mix 2 measures crème de cacao, 1 measure rum, 3 measures milk.

Passion Juice Mix 1 measure vodka to 3 measures passion fruit juice.

Tropical Sunset Mix 1 measure vodka to 2 measures tropical fruit juice. Add a piece of pineapple, a cherry and a twist of lime on a cocktail stick.

Not so Strong…
Cider Refresher Mix 2 measures dry cider to 1 measure orange juice.

Spritzer Half white wine to half sparkling mineral water.

Non-Alcoholic
Flaming Sunset Half-fill a glass with sweetened cranberry juice drink. Top up with tonic water or sparkling mineral water.

Bitter Fruits Shake several dashes of bitters into a glass. Top up with chilled sparkling unsweetened white grape juice. Add a slice of lemon and a maraschino or glacé cherry on a cocktail umbrella.

DIPS, NIBBLES & PÂTÉS

Dips with tasty nibbles and crudités to dunk in them are perfect party food – serve them either as an appetizer, or as one of several different party foods. They are especially easy to eat – no plates or forks required! Pâtés are also good – they can be prepared ahead and are delicious served with chunks of crusty French bread, or spread on either crackers or fingers of toast.

Aubergine Sunflower Pâté

INGREDIENTS

Serves 4
1 large aubergine
1 garlic clove, crushed
15ml/1 tbsp lemon juice
30ml/2 tbsp sunflower seeds
45ml/3 tbsp natural low fat yogurt
handful fresh coriander or parsley
black pepper
black olives, to garnish

1 Cut the aubergine in half and place, cut-side down, on a baking sheet. Place under a hot grill for 15–20 minutes, until the skin is blackened and the flesh is soft. Leave for a few minutes, to cool slightly.

2 Scoop the flesh of the aubergine into a food processor. Add the garlic, lemon juice, sunflower seeds, and yogurt. Process until smooth.

3 Coarsely chop the fresh coriander or parsley and mix in. Season, then spoon into a serving dish. Top with olives and serve with vegetable sticks.

——— COOK'S TIP ———
Instead of using this pâté as a dip, you could spread it on to crackers or rounds of toasted bread instead.

Pepper Dips with Crudités

Make one or both of these colourful vegetable dips – if you have time to make both they look spectacular together.

INGREDIENTS

Serves 4–6
2 medium red peppers, halved and seeded
2 medium yellow peppers, halved and seeded
2 garlic cloves
30ml/2 tbsp lemon juice
20ml/4 tsp olive oil
50g/2oz/½ cup fresh white breadcrumbs
salt and black pepper
fresh vegetables, for dipping

1 Place the peppers in separate saucepans with a peeled clove of garlic. Add just enough water to cover.

2 Bring to the boil, then cover and simmer for 15 minutes until tender. Drain, cool, then purée separately in a food processor or blender, adding half the lemon juice and olive oil to each.

3 Stir half the breadcrumbs into each and season to taste with salt and pepper. Serve the dips with a selection of fresh vegetables for dipping.

——— COOK'S TIP ———
You could make these dips up to 2 days in advance, transfer to an airtight container and chill until ready to eat.

Celeriac Fritters with Mustard Dip

The combination of the hot, crispy fritters and cold mustard dip is extremely good.

INGREDIENTS

Serves 4

1 egg
115g/4oz/1½ cups ground almonds
45ml/3 tbsp freshly grated Parmesan cheese
45ml/3 tbsp chopped fresh parsley
1 medium celeriac, about 450g/1lb
lemon juice
oil, for deep-frying
150ml/¼ pint/⅔ cup soured cream
15–30ml/1–2 tbsp wholegrain mustard
salt and black pepper
sea salt flakes, for sprinkling

1 Beat the egg well and pour into a shallow dish. Mix together the almonds, grated Parmesan and parsley in a separate dish. Season with salt and plenty of pepper. Set aside.

2 Peel and cut the celeriac into strips about 1cm/½in wide and 5cm/2in long. Drop them immediately into a bowl of water with a little lemon juice added to prevent discoloration.

3 Heat the oil to 180°C/350°F. Drain and then pat dry half the celeriac chips. Dip them into the beaten egg, then into the ground almond mixture, making sure that the pieces are coated completely and evenly.

4 Deep-fry the celeriac fritters, a few at a time, for 2–3 minutes until golden. Drain on kitchen paper and keep warm while you cook the remainder.

5 Meanwhile, to make the mustard dip, mix together the soured cream, mustard and salt to taste. Spoon into a small serving bowl.

6 Heap the celeriac fritters on to warmed serving plates. Sprinkle with sea salt flakes and serve at once with the mustard dip.

Mexican Dip with Chilli Chips

INGREDIENTS

Serves 4

2 medium ripe avocados
juice of 1 lime
½ small onion, finely chopped
½ red chilli, seeded and finely chopped
3 tomatoes, skinned, seeded and
  chopped
30ml/2 tbsp chopped fresh coriander
30ml/2 tbsp soured cream
salt and black pepper
15ml/1 tbsp soured cream and a pinch
  of cayenne pepper, to garnish

For the chips

150g/5oz bag tortilla chips
30ml/2 tbsp finely grated mature
  Cheddar cheese
1.25ml/¼ tsp chilli powder
10ml/2 tbsp chopped fresh parsley

1 Halve and stone the avocados and remove the flesh with a spoon, scraping the shells well.

2 Place the flesh in a blender or food processor with the remaining ingredients and pulse until fairly smooth. Transfer to a bowl, cover and chill.

3 Meanwhile, preheat the grill, then scatter the tortilla chips over a baking sheet. Mix the grated cheese with the chilli powder, sprinkle over the chips and grill for 1–2 minutes, until the cheese has melted.

4 Remove the avocado dip from the fridge, top with the soured cream and sprinkle with cayenne pepper. Serve the bowl on a plate surrounded by the tortilla chips sprinkled with the fresh parsley.

Raw Vegetables with Olive Oil Dip

Use a combination of any fresh vegetables for this colourful antipasto from Rome, where the dip usually consists only of olive oil and salt.

INGREDIENTS

Serves 6–8
3 large carrots, peeled
2 fennel bulbs
6 celery sticks
1 pepper
12 radishes, trimmed
2 large tomatoes, or 12 cherry tomatoes
8 spring onions
12 small cauliflower florets

For the dip
125ml/4fl oz/½ cup extra virgin olive oil
45ml/3 tbsp fresh lemon juice (optional)
4 fresh basil leaves, torn into small
    pieces (optional)
salt and black pepper

1 Prepare the vegetables by slicing the carrots, fennel, celery and pepper into small sticks.

2 Cut the large tomatoes into sections if using. Trim the roots and dark green leaves from the spring onions. Arrange the vegetables on a large platter, leaving space in the centre for the dip.

3 Make the dip by pouring the olive oil into a small bowl. Add salt and pepper. Stir in the lemon juice and basil, if using. Place the bowl in the centre of the vegetable platter.

Celery Stuffed with Gorgonzola

These are very easy to make and perfect for serving with drinks.

INGREDIENTS

Serves 4–6
12 crisp celery sticks, leaves left on
75g/3oz/½ cup Gorgonzola cheese
75g/3oz/½ cup cream cheese
fresh chives, to garnish

1 Wash and dry the celery sticks and trim the root ends.

2 In a small bowl, mash the cheeses together until smooth.

3 Fill the celery sticks with the cheese mixture, using a palette knife to smooth the filling. Chill before serving. Garnish with snipped chives.

COOK'S TIP

Use another soft and creamy blue cheese in place of the Gorgonzola, if you prefer – or choose a strong flavoured Cheddar and grate finely before adding to the cream cheese.

Goat's Cheese Dip with Herbs

INGREDIENTS

Makes about 475ml/16fl oz

275g/10oz soft mild goat's cheese
120ml/4fl oz/½ cup single cream
10ml/2 tsp fresh lemon juice
15ml/1 tbsp chopped fresh chives
15ml/1 tbsp chopped fresh parsley
30ml/2 tbsp chopped fresh basil
black pepper
raw or briefly cooked cold vegetables,
  crisps or crackers, for serving

1 In a food processor or blender, combine the goat's cheese and cream and process to blend. Add the lemon juice and process until smooth.

2 Scrape into a bowl. Stir in the chives, parsley, basil, and pepper to taste. Serve cold, as a dip for vegetables, crisps, or crackers.

Tangy Avocado Dip

INGREDIENTS

Makes about 350ml/12fl oz

30ml/2 tbsp wine vinegar
2.5ml/½ tsp salt, or to taste
4ml/¾ tsp white pepper
½ red onion, coarsely chopped
45ml/3 tbsp olive oil
1 large ripe avocado, halved and stone
  removed
15ml/1 tbsp fresh lemon juice
45ml/3 tbsp natural yogurt
45ml/3 tbsp water, or as needed
30ml/2 tbsp chopped fresh coriander
raw or briefly cooked cold vegetables,
  for serving

--- COOK'S TIP ---

This versatile dip need not be limited to serving with salads and crudités. Serve it as a sauce with grilled chicken or fish, or use it on sandwiches in place of mayonnaise or mustard, or to provide a cool contrast to any sort of spicy food.

1 In a bowl, combine the vinegar and salt and stir with a fork to dissolve. Stir in the pepper, chopped red onion, and olive oil.

3 Add the yogurt and water and process until smooth. If desired, add more water to thin. Taste and adjust the seasoning if necessary.

2 Scoop the avocado flesh into a food processor or blender. Add the lemon juice and onion dressing and process just to blend.

4 Scrape into a bowl. Stir in the coriander. Serve immediately, as a dressing for salads, or use as a dip for raw or briefly cooked cold vegetables.

Chicken Liver Pâté with Marsala

This is a really quick and simple pâté to make, yet it has a delicious – and quite sophisticated – flavour. It contains Marsala, a soft and pungent fortified wine from Sicily. If it is unavailable, use brandy or a medium-dry sherry.

INGREDIENTS

Serves 4

350g/12oz chicken livers, defrosted
  if frozen
225g/8oz/1 cup butter, softened
2 garlic cloves, crushed
15ml/1 tbsp Marsala
5ml/1 tsp chopped fresh sage
salt and black pepper
8 sage leaves, to garnish
Melba toast, to serve

1 Pick over the chicken livers, then rinse and dry with kitchen paper. Melt 25g/1oz/2 tbsp of the butter in a frying pan, and fry the chicken livers with the garlic over a medium heat for about 5 minutes, or until they are firm but still pink in the middle.

2 Transfer the livers to a blender or food processor, using a slotted spoon, and add the Marsala and chopped sage.

3 Melt 150g/5oz/10 tbsp of the remaining butter in the frying pan, stirring to loosen any sediment, then pour into the blender or processor and blend until smooth. Season well.

4 Spoon the pâté into four individual pots and smooth the surface. Melt the remaining butter in a separate pan and pour over the pâtés. Garnish with sage leaves and chill until set. Serve with triangles of Melba toast.

Ploughman's Pâté

INGREDIENTS

Serves 4

50g/2oz/3 tbsp full fat soft cheese
50g/2oz/¾ cup grated Caerphilly cheese
50g/2oz/¾ cup grated Double
   Gloucester cheese
4 silverskin pickled onions, drained and
   finely chopped
15ml/1 tbsp apricot chutney
25g/1oz/2 tbsp butter, melted
30ml/2 tbsp snipped fresh chives
salt and black pepper
4 slices soft grain bread
watercress and cherry tomatoes,
   to serve

1 Mix together the soft cheese, grated cheeses, onions, chutney and butter in a bowl and season lightly.

2 Spoon the mixture on to a sheet of greaseproof paper and roll up into a cylinder, smoothing the mixture into a roll with your hands. Scrunch the ends of the paper together and twist to seal. Pop in the freezer for about 30 minutes, until just firm.

3 Spread the chives on a plate, then unwrap the chilled cheese pâté. Roll in the chives until evenly coated. Wrap in clear film and chill for 10 minutes.

4 Preheat the grill. Toast the bread lightly on both sides. Cut off the crusts and slice each piece in half horizontally. Cut each half into two triangles. Grill, untoasted side up, until golden and curled at the edges.

5 Slice the pâté into rounds and serve three or four rounds per person with the Melba toast, watercress and cherry tomatoes.

Chicken, Bacon and Walnut Terrine

INGREDIENTS

Serves 8–10

2 boneless chicken breast portions
1 large garlic clove, crushed
½ slice bread
1 egg
350g/12oz bacon chops (the fattier the
   better), minced or finely chopped
225g/8oz chicken or turkey livers,
   finely chopped
25g/1oz/¼ cup chopped walnuts,
   toasted
30ml/2 tbsp sweet sherry or Madeira
2.5ml/½ tsp ground allspice
2.5ml/½ tsp cayenne pepper
pinch each ground nutmeg and
   cloves
8 long rashers streaky bacon, rinded
   and stretched
salt and black pepper
chicory leaves and chives, to garnish

1 Cut the chicken breasts into thin strips and season lightly. Mash the garlic, bread and egg together. Work in the chopped bacon (using your hands is really the best way) and then the finely chopped livers. Stir in the chopped walnuts, sherry or Madeira, spices, and seasoning to taste.

2 Preheat the oven to 200°C/400°F/ Gas 6. Line a 675g/1½ lb loaf tin with the bacon rashers and pack in half the meat mixture. Lay the chicken strips on the top and spread the rest of the mixture over. Cover the loaf tin with lightly greased foil, seal well and press down firmly.

3 Place the terrine in a roasting tin half full of hot water and bake for 1–1½ hours, or until firm to the touch. Remove from the oven and place weights on the top and leave to cool completely. Drain off any excess fat or liquid while the terrine is warm.

4 When really cold, turn out the terrine, cut into thick slices and serve at once, garnished with a few chicory leaves and chives.

COOK'S TIP

If you wish to seal the terrine for longer storage, pour melted lard over, while it is still in its tin. Leave to set and form a complete seal.

Blinis with Smoked Salmon and Dill Cream

INGREDIENTS

Serves 4

115g/4oz/1 cup buckwheat flour
115g/4oz/1 cup plain flour
pinch of salt
15ml/1 tbsp easy-blend dried yeast
2 eggs
350ml/12fl oz/1½ cups warm milk
15ml/1 tbsp melted butter, plus extra
    for frying
150ml/¼ pint/⅔ cup crème fraîche
45ml/3 tbsp chopped fresh dill
225g/8oz smoked salmon,
    thinly sliced
fresh dill sprigs, to garnish

1 Mix together the buckwheat and plain flours in a large bowl with the salt. Sprinkle in the yeast and mix well. Separate one of the eggs. Whisk together the whole egg and the yolk, the warm milk and the melted butter.

2 Pour the egg mixture on to the flour mixture. Beat well to form a smooth batter. Cover with clear film and leave to rise in a warm place for 1–2 hours.

3 Whisk the remaining egg white in a large bowl until it holds stiff peaks, then gently fold into the batter.

4 Preheat a heavy-based frying pan or griddle and brush with melted butter. Drop tablespoons of the batter on to the pan, spacing them well apart. Cook for about 40 seconds, until bubbles appear on the surface.

5 Flip over the blinis and cook for 30 seconds on the other side. Wrap in foil and keep warm in a low oven. Repeat with the remaining mixture, buttering the pan each time.

6 Mix together the crème fraîche and dill. Serve the blinis topped with the smoked salmon and dill cream. Garnish with sprigs of fresh dill.

Stuffed Devilled Eggs

INGREDIENTS

Serves 6

6 hard boiled eggs, peeled
60ml/4 tbsp minced cooked ham
6 walnut halves, finely chopped
15ml/1 tbsp finely chopped spring
   onion
15ml/1 tbsp Dijon mustard
15ml/1 tbsp mayonnaise
10ml/2 tsp white wine or tarragon
   vinegar
large pinch of cayenne pepper
salt and black pepper
paprika and a few slices of dill pickle,
   for garnishing

1 Cut each egg in half lengthways. Place the yolks in a bowl and set the white aside.

2 Mash the yolks well with a fork, or push them through a strainer. Add all the remaining ingredients and mix well with the yolks. Taste and adjust the seasoning if necessary.

3 Spoon the filling into the egg white halves, or pipe it in with a piping bag and nozzle. Garnish the top of each stuffed egg with a little paprika and a small star or other shape cut from the pickle slices. Serve the stuffed eggs at room temperature.

Nut and Cheese Stuffed Celery Sticks

INGREDIENTS

Serves 4–6

12 crisp, tender celery sticks
25g/1oz/¼ cup crumbled blue cheese
115g/4oz/½ cup cream cheese
45ml/3 tbsp soured cream
50g/2oz/½ cup chopped walnuts

2 In a small bowl, combine the crumbled blue cheese, cream cheese, and sour cream. Stir together with a wooden spoon until smoothly blended. Fold in all but 15ml/1 tbsp of the chopped walnuts.

3 Fill the celery pieces with the cheese mixture. Chill before serving, garnished with the reserved walnuts.

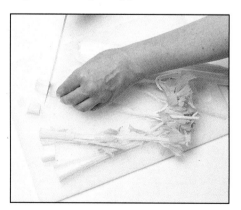

1 Trim the celery sticks and cut into 10cm/4in pieces.

— VARIATION —

Use the same filling to stuff scooped out cherry tomatoes.

Chicory with Cheese and Peppers

Calorie counters can tuck into this crunchy treat. Serve as finger eats at a drinks party.

INGREDIENTS

Makes about 16
2 large heads of chicory
115g/4oz/½ cup low fat cream or curd cheese
15ml/1 tbsp thick natural yogurt
1 garlic clove, crushed
30ml/2 tbsp chopped sun-dried tomatoes, preserved in oil, drained
30ml/2 tbsp seeded and chopped red pepper
15ml/1 tbsp snipped fresh chives
15ml/1 tbsp chopped fresh basil
salt and black pepper
shredded red pepper, to garnish

1 Trim the chicory and carefully separate the leaves. Arrange on a large platter or serving dish.

3 Put a teaspoonful of the filling in each chicory leaf, at the stalk end, and garnish with the shredded pepper.

2 Blend or beat together the cheese, yogurt and garlic. Add the tomato, pepper and herbs, and season to taste.

COOK'S TIP

Celery would be just as good if chicory is not available.

Chicken and Avocado Mayonnaise

You need quite firm 'scoops' to eat this dip, so if you pass it round as finger food don't use ordinary crisps for dipping.

INGREDIENTS

Serves 4
30ml/2 tbsp mayonnaise
15ml/1 tbsp fromage frais
2 garlic cloves, crushed
115g/4oz/1 cup chopped cooked chicken
1 large ripe, but firm, avocado, peeled and stoned
30ml/2 tbsp lemon juice
salt and black pepper
nacho chips or tortilla chips, to serve

1 Mix together the mayonnaise, fromage frais, garlic, and seasoning. to taste, in a small bowl. Stir in the chopped chicken.

2 Chop the avocado and immediately toss in lemon juice, then mix gently into the chicken mixture. Check the seasoning and chill until required.

3 Serve in small serving dishes with the chips as scoops.

COOK'S TIP

This mixture also makes a great, chunky filling for sandwiches, baps or pitta bread. Or serve as a main course salad, heaped on to a base of mixed salad leaves.

HOT FINGER FOOD

Hot nibbles are delicious and extremely moreish. The simplest can be prepared ahead, then baked at the last moment – try Chinese Chicken Wings, Mushroom Popovers or Nut Patties with Mango Relish. If you are cooking for a crowd, try deep frying fritters, croquettes and goujons early in the day, then reheating and crisping them in the oven just before you serve them.

Mushroom Croustades

The rich mushroom flavour of this filling is heightened by the addition of Worcestershire sauce.

INGREDIENTS 🍎

Serves 2–4

1 short baguette, about 25cm/10in
10ml/2 tsp olive oil
250g/9oz open cup mushrooms, quartered
10ml/2 tsp Worcestershire sauce
10ml/2 tsp lemon juice
30ml/2 tbsp skimmed milk
30ml/2 tbsp snipped fresh chives
salt and black pepper
snipped fresh chives, to garnish

1 Preheat the oven to 200°C/400°F/ Gas 6. Cut the baguette in half lengthways. Cut a scoop out of the soft middle of each using a sharp knife, leaving a thick border all the way around.

2 Brush the bread with oil, place on a baking sheet, and bake for about 6–8 minutes, until golden and crisp.

3 Place the mushrooms in a small saucepan with the Worcestershire sauce, lemon juice, and milk. Simmer for about 5 minutes, or until most of the liquid is evaporated.

4 Remove from the heat, then add the chives and seasoning. Spoon into the bread croustades and serve hot, garnished with snipped chives.

COOK'S TIP

This is an ideal way of using up French bread that is one or two days old, but make sure you don't bake it too long, or it may become too crisp to eat!

Tomato and Pesto Toasties

Ready-made pesto is high in fat but, as its flavour is so powerful, it can be used in very small amounts with good effect, as in these tasty toasties.

INGREDIENTS 🍎

Serves 2
2 thick slices crusty bread
45ml/3 tbsp low fat cream cheese or
   low fat fromage frais
10ml/2 tsp red or green pesto
1 beefsteak tomato
1 red onion
salt and black pepper

1 Place the bread slices under a hot grill until golden brown on both sides, turning once. Leave to cool.

2 Mix together the low fat cream cheese or fromage frais and pesto in a small bowl until well blended, then spread thickly on the toasted bread.

3 Cut the beefsteak tomato and red onion, crossways, into thin slices using a large sharp knife.

4 Arrange the slices, overlapping, on top of the toast and season with salt and pepper. Transfer the toasties to a grill pan and grill until heated through, then serve immediately.

—— COOK'S TIP ——

Almost any type of crusty bread can be used for this recipe, but Italian olive oil bread and French bread will give the best flavour.

—— VARIATION ——

To make Cheese-topped Toasties, sprinkle a little finely grated Parmesan or another hard, flavourful cheese over the sliced tomatoes before grilling.

Pork and Prawn Toasts

A popular starter in China and Thailand. Serve the toasts piping hot with a bowl of sweet chilli dipping sauce.

INGREDIENTS

Serves 4

115g/4oz minced pork
115g/4oz/1 cup peeled cooked prawns
1 garlic clove, crushed
2 spring onions, finely chopped
30ml/2 tbsp, chopped fresh coriander
1 egg white, lightly beaten
5ml/1 tsp light soy sauce
5ml/1 tsp grated lemon rind
4 slices white bread, crusts removed
60ml/4 tbsp sesame seeds
oil, for frying
lemon wedges, to serve
fresh coriander sprigs, to garnish

1 Place the pork, prawns, garlic, spring onions, coriander, egg white, soy sauce and lemon rind in a food processor or blender and pulse until the mixture is fairly smooth.

2 Flatten the bread slices with a rolling pin, then spread about 5mm/¼in of the pork and prawn mixture on each slice, pressing down well. Cut each slice of bread into four triangles.

3 Sprinkle the sesame seeds in a shallow bowl and coat the triangles meat-side down with the seeds.

4 Heat 1cm/½in oil in a frying pan until a cube of bread browns in 30 seconds. Fry the toasts meat side down for 3–4 minutes, then turn them over and fry for 2 minutes. Drain on kitchen paper and serve hot, with lemon wedges, and coriander, to garnish.

Mediterranean Garlic Toast

Mediterranean garlic toast, or *bruschetta*, is served as an appetizer in Spain, Greece and Italy. With a topping of plum tomatoes, mozzarella cheese and salami, it makes a filling snack.

INGREDIENTS

Serves 4

150g/5oz mozzarella cheese, drained
2 plum tomatoes
½ French loaf
1 garlic clove, halved
30ml/2 tbsp olive oil, plus extra for brushing
12 small salami slices
15ml/1 tbsp fresh torn basil, or 5ml/1 tsp dried basil
salt and black pepper
fresh basil sprigs, to garnish

1 Preheat the grill to a medium heat. Cut the mozzarella cheese into twelve slices and each tomato into six slices. Cut the French bread in half and slice each half horizontally.

2 Place the bread under the grill, cut side up, and toast lightly. While the bread is still warm, rub the cut sides of the garlic clove on each cut side of the bread, then drizzle over about 7.5ml/½ tbsp of the olive oil.

3 Top each toast with three slices of tomato, three slices of mozzarella and three slices of salami. Brush the tops with a little more olive oil, season well and sprinkle over the basil.

4 Return to the grill and toast for 2–3 minutes, until the cheese has melted. Remove and serve hot, garnished with sprigs of fresh basil.

Crostini with Cheese

These Italian nibbles can be made with various toppings, and are served hot or cold with drinks. This cheese-topped version is always popular.

INGREDIENTS

Serves 6
4–6 slices day-old white or brown bread
75g/3oz/¾ cup thinly sliced cheese (such as Cheddar or gruyère)
anchovy fillets
strips of grilled red pepper
freshly ground black pepper

1 Cut the bread into small shapes (triangle, circle, oval, etc.). Preheat the oven to 190°C/375°F/Gas 5.

2 Place a thin slice of cheese on each piece of bread, cutting it to fit.

3 Cut the anchovy fillets and strips of pepper into small decorative shapes and place on top of the cheese. Grind a little pepper on each.

4 Butter a baking sheet. Place the crostini on it, and bake for 10 minutes, or until the cheese has melted. Serve straight from the oven, or allow to cool before serving if you prefer.

--------- COOK'S TIP ---------

For a colourful addition use strips of green or yellow pepper.

Crostini with Mussels

Each of these seafood crostini is topped with a mussel and then baked. Use fresh seafood whenever possible.

INGREDIENTS

Makes 16

16 large mussels, in their shells
4 large slices bread, 2.5cm/1in thick
40g/1½oz/3 tbsp butter
30ml/2 tbsp chopped fresh parsley
1 shallot, very finely chopped
olive oil, for brushing
lemon wedges, to serve

3 Break the scooped-out bread into crumbs, and reserve. In a small frying pan, heat the butter, add the parsley, shallot and the reserved breadcrumbs and cook until the shallot softens.

4 Brush each piece of bread with olive oil. Place one mussel in each hollow. Spoon a small amount of the parsley and shallot mixture onto each mussel. Place on an oiled baking sheet and bake for 10 minutes. Serve at once, while still hot, with the lemon wedges.

1 Wash the mussels well in several changes of water. Pull the 'beards' off the mussels. Place the mussels in a saucepan with a cupful of water, and heat until the shells open. (Discard any that do not open.) As soon as they open, lift the mussels out of the pan. Spoon out of their shells, and set aside. Preheat the oven to 190°C/375°F/Gas 5.

2 Cut off the crusts from the bread and cut each slice into quarters. Scoop out a hollow from the top of each piece large enough to hold a mussel. Do not cut through to the bottom.

Sweetcorn and Bacon Fritters

INGREDIENTS

Makes 8

200g/7oz/1¼ cups canned sweetcorn, drained well
2 eggs, separated
90ml/6 tbsp plain flour
75ml/5 tbsp milk
1 small courgette, grated
2 rindless back bacon rashers, diced
2 spring onions, finely chopped
a good pinch of cayenne pepper
45ml/3 tbsp sunflower oil
salt and black pepper
fresh coriander sprigs, to garnish

For the salsa

3 tomatoes, skinned, seeded and diced
½ small red pepper, seeded and diced
½ small onion, diced
15ml/1 tbsp lemon juice
15ml/1 tbsp chopped fresh coriander
dash of Tabasco sauce
salt and black pepper

1 To make the salsa, place all the ingredients in a bowl, mix well and season. Cover and chill.

2 Empty the sweetcorn into a bowl and mix in the egg yolks. Add the flour and blend in with a wooden spoon. When the mixture thickens, gradually blend in the milk.

3 Stir in the courgette, bacon, spring onions, cayenne pepper and seasoning and set aside.

4 Place the egg whites in a clean bowl and whisk until stiff. Gently fold into the sweetcorn batter mixture with a metal spoon.

5 Heat 30ml/2 tbsp of the oil in a large frying pan and place four large spoonfuls of the mixture into the oil. Fry on a moderate heat for 2–3 minutes on each side until golden, then drain on kitchen paper. Keep warm in the oven while frying the remaining four fritters, adding 15ml/1 tbsp oil if necessary.

6 Serve two fritters each, garnished with coriander sprigs and a spoonful of the chilled tomato salsa.

Rice and Cheese Croquettes

Although you can use leftover cooked rice here, freshly cooked rice is easier to work with. The garlicky mayonnaise aïoli makes a good dip for crudités too.

INGREDIENTS

Makes about 16

115g/4oz/1½ cups long grain rice, cooked
2 eggs, lightly beaten
75g/3oz mozzarella or Bel Paese cheese, grated
50g/2oz/½ cup fine dry breadcrumbs
salt and black pepper
oil, for frying

For the aïoli

1 egg yolk
few drops of lemon juice or vinegar
1 large garlic clove, crushed
250ml/8 floz/1 cup good salad oil

1 Drain the cooked rice thoroughly and allow to cool slightly, then mix in the eggs, cheese and seasoning.

2 Mould the rice mixture with your hands into 16 equal sized balls and coat in breadcrumbs, pressing on the crumbs well. Chill for 20 minutes.

3 Meanwhile, make the aïoli; beat together the egg yolk, lemon juice, garlic and seasoning. Gradually whisk in sufficient oil to give a thick, glossy mayonnaise. Chill until ready to serve.

4 Heat the oil in a frying pan until almost hazy, then cook the rice balls, in two batches, for 4–5 minutes each, or until crisp and golden all over.

5 Drain the rice balls on kitchen paper as soon as they are cooked and keep warm until required (or reheat in a hot oven) before serving with the garlic dip.

> ——— COOK'S TIP ———
>
> These are very good if you give them a surprise centre – try ham, olives or nuts.

Fried Fish Goujons

INGREDIENTS

Serves 4

60ml/4 tbsp mayonnaise
30ml/2 tbsp natural yogurt
grated rind of ½ lemon
squeeze of lemon juice
15ml/1 tbsp chopped fresh parsley
15ml/1 tbsp capers, chopped
2 x 175g/6oz sole fillets, skinned
2 x 175g/6oz plaice fillets, skinned
1 egg, lightly beaten
115g/4oz/2 cups fresh white breadcrumbs
15ml/1 tbsp sesame seeds
pinch of paprika
salt and black pepper
oil, for frying
4 lemon wedges, to serve
watercress, to garnish

1 To make the lemon mayonnaise, mix together the mayonnaise, yogurt, lemon rind and juice, parsley and capers in a bowl. Cover and chill.

2 Cut the fish fillets into thin strips. Place the beaten egg in one shallow bowl. In another bowl, mix together the breadcrumbs, sesame seeds, paprika and seasoning.

3 Dip the fish strips, one at a time, into the beaten egg, then into the breadcrumb mixture and toss until coated evenly. Lay on a clean plate.

4 Heat about 2.5cm/1in of oil in a frying pan until a cube of bread browns in 30 seconds. Deep-fry the strips in batches for 2–3 minutes, until lightly golden.

5 Remove with a slotted spoon, drain on kitchen paper and keep warm in the oven while frying the remainder. Garnish with watercress and serve hot with lemon wedges and the chilled lemon mayonnaise.

--- COOK'S TIP ---

Use any white fish fillets for the goujons – just be sure to cut them into thin strips. You could try a mixture of haddock and cod as an alternative to the sole and plaice.

Garlic Chilli Prawns

In Spain *Gambas al Ajillo* are traditionally cooked in small earthenware dishes, but a frying pan is just as good.

INGREDIENTS

Serves 4

60ml/4 tbsp olive oil
2–3 garlic cloves, finely chopped
½–1 fresh red chilli, seeded and
   chopped
16 cooked whole Mediterranean
   prawns
15ml/1 tbsp chopped fresh parsley
salt and black pepper
lemon wedges and French bread,
   to serve

1 Heat the oil in a large frying pan and add the garlic and chilli. Stir-fry for 1 minute, until the garlic begins to turn brown.

2 Add the Mediterranean prawns and stir-fry for 3–4 minutes, coating them well with the flavoured oil.

3 Add the parsley, remove from the heat and serve four prawns per person in heated bowls, with the flavoured oil spooned over them. Serve with lemon wedges for squeezing and French bread to mop up the juices.

Chinese Chicken Wings

INGREDIENTS

Serves 4

75ml/5 tbsp soy sauce
15ml/1 tbsp light brown sugar
15ml/1 tbsp rice vinegar
30ml/1 tbsp dry sherry wine
juice of 1 orange
strip of orange peel
1 star anise
5ml/1 tsp cornflour
50ml/2fl oz/¼ cup water
15ml/1 tbsp fresh root ginger
2.5–5ml/½–1 tsp oriental chilli-garlic
    sauce, to taste
22–24 chicken wings, tips removed

1 Preheat the oven to 200°C/400°F/ Gas 6. Combine the soy sauce, brown sugar, vinegar, sherry, orange juice and peel, and star anise in a saucepan. Bring to the boil.

2 Combine the cornflour and water in a small bowl and stir until blended. Add to the boiling soy sauce mixture, stirring well. Boil for 1 minute more, stirring constantly.

3 Remove the soy sauce mixture from the heat and stir in the grated ginger and chilli-garlic sauce.

4 Arrange the chicken wings, in one layer, in a large baking dish. Pour over the soy sauce mixture and stir to coat the wings evenly.

5 Bake until tender and browned, 30–40 minutes, basting occasionally. Serve the wings hot or warm.

Spinach-stuffed Mushrooms

INGREDIENTS

Serves 4

275g/10oz spinach, stalks removed
400g/14oz medium cap mushrooms
25g/1oz/2 tbsp butter, plus extra for
  brushing
25g/1oz bacon, chopped
½ small onion, finely chopped
75ml/5 tbsp double cream
about 60ml/4 tbsp finely grated
  Cheddar cheese
30ml/2 tbsp fresh breadcrumbs
salt and black pepper
sprig of parsley, to garnish

1 Preheat the oven to 190°C/375°F/
Gas 5. Butter a baking dish. Wash
but do not dry the spinach. Place it in
a pan and cook, stirring occasionally,
until wilted and no liquid is visible.

2 Tip the spinach into a colander and
squeeze out as much liquid as
possible. Chop finely. Snap the stalks
from the mushrooms and chop the
stalks finely.

3 Melt the butter, then cook the
bacon, onion and mushroom stalks
for about 5 minutes. Stir in the
spinach, cook for a moment or two,
then remove the pan from the heat and
stir in the cream and seasoning.

4 Brush the mushroom caps with
melted butter, then place, gills
uppermost, in a single layer in the
baking dish.

5 Divide the spinach mixture among
the mushrooms. Mix together the
cheese and breadcrumbs, sprinkle over
the mushrooms, then bake for about
20 minutes, until the mushrooms are
tender. Serve warm, garnished with a
sprig of parsley.

WATCHPOINT

It is important to make sure that all the sur-
plus liquid is squeezed out of the spinach,
otherwise the stuffing will be too soggy.

Mushroom Popovers

Popovers are a delicious party snack – make them large, like these ones, or bake the batter in bun tins to make mini popovers. You could add sweetcorn and chopped tomato or ham to the filling.

INGREDIENTS

Serves 4
1 egg
115g/4oz/1 cup plain flour
300ml/½ pint/1¼ cups milk
pinch salt

For the filling
15ml/1 tbsp sunflower oil
115g/4oz mushrooms, sliced
few drops lemon juice
10ml/2 tsp chopped fresh parsley
  or thyme
¼ red pepper, seeded and chopped
salt and black pepper
fresh basil leaves, to garnish

1 To make the popovers, whisk the egg and flour together and gradually add a little milk to blend, then whisk in the rest of the milk to make a smooth batter. Add a pinch of salt and leave the batter to stand for 10–20 minutes.

2 When required, preheat the oven to 190°C/425°F/Gas 7. Pour very little oil into the base of eight Yorkshire pudding tins and heat through in the oven for 4–5 minutes. Pour the batter into the very hot tins and cook for 20 minutes or until well risen and crispy.

3 Meanwhile, make the filling; heat the oil and sauté the mushrooms with the lemon juice, herbs and seasoning until most of their liquid has evaporated. Add the red pepper at the last minute so that it keeps its crunch. Season to taste.

4 To serve, spoon the filling into the hot popover cases and scatter over the basil leaves.

Tuna Fishcake Bites

Canned salmon could also be used for these tasty nibbles.

INGREDIENTS

Serves 4
675g/1½lb (about 5 medium) potatoes
knob of butter
2 hard-boiled eggs, chopped
3 spring onions, finely chopped
finely grated rind of ½ lemon
5ml/1 tsp lemon juice
30ml/2 tbsp chopped fresh parsley
200g/7oz can tuna in oil, drained
10ml/2 tsp capers, chopped
2 eggs, lightly beaten
115g/4oz/2 cups fresh white breadcrumbs, for coating
sunflower oil, for frying
salt and black pepper
mixed salad, to serve

For the tartare sauce
60ml/4 tbsp mayonnaise
15ml/1 tbsp natural yogurt
15ml/1 tbsp finely chopped gherkins
15ml/1 tbsp capers, chopped
15ml/1 tbsp chopped fresh parsley

1 Cook the potatoes in a pan of boil-ing salted water until tender. Drain well, add the butter and mash well. Leave to cool.

2 Add the hard-boiled eggs, spring onions, lemon rind, lemon juice, parsley, tuna, capers and 15ml/1 tbsp of the beaten egg to the cooled potato. Mix well with a fork and season. Cover and chill for about 30 minutes.

3 Meanwhile, place all the ingredients for the tartare sauce in a bowl and mix well. Chill and reserve.

4 Pour the remaining beaten egg into one shallow bowl and the bread-crumbs into another. Roll the chilled fishcake mixture into about 24 balls. Dip these into the egg and then roll gently in the breadcrumbs until evenly coated. Transfer to a plate.

5 Heat 90ml/6 tbsp of oil in a frying pan and fry the balls on a moderate heat, in batches, for about 4 minutes, turning two or three times until browned all over. Drain on kitchen paper and keep warm in the oven while frying the remainder.

6 Serve the fishcake bites with the tartare sauce and salad.

Salmon and Prawn Fritters

INGREDIENTS

Serves 4

½ fennel bulb, cut in pieces
1 medium leek, cut in pieces
1 green pepper, seeded and cut
  in pieces
2 garlic cloves
15ml/1 tbsp butter
pinch of dried red pepper flakes
175g/6oz skinless boneless salmon, cut
  in pieces
100g/3½oz skinless boneless cod or
  haddock, cut in pieces
75g/3oz peeled, cooked prawns
115g/4oz flour
6 eggs, beaten
350–475ml/12–16fl oz milk
15ml/1 tbsp chopped fresh basil
60–90ml/4–6 tbsp oil, for greasing
salt and black pepper
soured cream, for serving

1 Combine the fennel, leek, pepper, and garlic in a food processor and process until finely chopped.

--- VARIATION ---

To make richer Salmon Fritters, increase the amount of salmon to 425g/15oz, and omit the cod or haddock and prawns. Use dill in place of the basil.

2 Melt the butter in a frying pan until sizzling. Add the vegetable mixture and red pepper flakes. Season with salt and pepper. Cook over a low heat until softened, 8–10 minutes. Remove from the heat and set aside.

3 Combine the salmon, cod or haddock, and prawns in the food processor. Process, using the pulse button and scraping the sides of the container several times, until the mixture is coarsely chopped. Scrape into a large bowl and set aside.

4 Sift the flour into another bowl and make a well in the centre.

5 Gradually whisk in the eggs alternately with 350ml/12fl oz of the milk to make a smooth batter. If necessary, strain the batter to remove lumps.

6 Stir the seafood, vegetables, and basil into the batter. If it seems too thick, add a little more milk.

7 Lightly oil a griddle or non-stick frying pan and heat over a medium heat. Add spoonfuls of the batter to the pan. Cook for 2–3 minutes until the fritters are golden around the edges. Turn them over and cook the other side for 2–3 minutes more. Work in batches, keeping the cooked fritters warm. Serve hot, with soured cream.

Nut Patties with Mango Relish

These spicy patties can be made in advance, if you like, and reheated just before serving.

INGREDIENTS

Serves 4–6
175g/6oz/1½ cups finely chopped
    roasted and salted cashew nuts
175g/6oz/1½ cups finely chopped
    walnuts
1 small onion, finely chopped
1 garlic clove, crushed
1 green chilli, seeded and chopped
5ml/1 tsp ground cumin
10ml/2 tsp ground coriander
2 carrots, coarsely grated
50g/2oz/1 cup fresh white bread-
    crumbs
30ml/2 tbsp chopped fresh coriander
15ml/1 tbsp lemon juice
1–2 eggs, beaten
salt and black pepper
coriander sprigs, to garnish

For the relish
1 large ripe mango, cut into small cubes
1 small onion, cut into slivers
5ml/1 tsp grated fresh root ginger
pinch of salt
15ml/1 tbsp sesame oil
5ml/1 tsp black mustard seeds

1 Preheat the oven to 180°C/350°F/ Gas 4. Mix together the nuts, onion, garlic, chilli, spices, carrots, breadcrumbs, chopped coriander and seasoning in a bowl.

2 Sprinkle over the lemon juice and add enough of the beaten egg to bind the mixture together. Shape the mixture into 12 balls, then flatten slightly into round patties.

3 Place the patties on a lightly greased baking tray and bake for about 25 minutes, until golden brown.

4 Meanwhile, to make the relish, mix together the mango, onion, fresh root ginger and salt.

5 Heat the oil in a small frying pan and add the mustard seeds. Fry for a few seconds until they pop, then stir into the mango mixture. Serve with the nut patties, garnished with coriander.

Parmesan Fish Goujons

Use this batter, with or without the cheese, whenever you feel brave enough to fry fish. This is light and crisp, just like fish and chip shop batter.

INGREDIENTS

Serves 4

375g/12oz plaice or sole fillets, or
   thicker fish such as cod or haddock
little flour
oil, for deep-frying
salt and black pepper
sprigs of dill, to garnish

For the cream sauce

60ml/4 tbsp soured cream
60ml/4 tbsp mayonnaise
2.5ml/½ tsp grated lemon rind
30ml/2 tbsp chopped gherkins or
   capers
15ml/1 tbsp chopped, mixed fresh
   herbs, or 5ml/1 tsp dried

For the batter

75g/3oz/¾ cup plain flour
25g/1oz/¼ cup Parmesan cheese
5ml/1 tsp bicarbonate of soda
1 egg, separated
150ml/¼ pint/⅔ cup milk

1 To make the cream sauce, mix the soured cream, mayonnaise, lemon rind, gherkins or capers, herbs and seasoning together, then chill.

2 To make the batter, sift the flour into a bowl. Mix in the other dry ingredients and salt, and then whisk in the egg yolk and milk to give a thick yet smooth batter. Then gradually whisk in 90ml/6 tbsp water. Season and chill.

3 Skin the fish and cut into thin strips of similar length. Season the flour and then dip the fish lightly in the flour.

4 Heat at least 5cm/2in oil in a large pan with a lid. Whisk the egg white until stiff and gently fold into the batter until just blended.

5 Dip the floured fish into the batter, drain off any excess and then drop gently into the hot fat.

6 Cook the fish in batches so that the goujons don't stick to one another, for only 3–4 minutes, turning once. When the batter is golden and crisp, remove the fish with a draining spoon. Place on kitchen paper on a plate in a warm oven while cooking the rest.

7 Serve hot with cream sauce or a bowl of mayonnaise for dipping.

Golden Cheese Puffs

Serve these deep-fried puffs –
called *aigrettes* in France – with
a fruity chutney and salad.

INGREDIENTS

Makes 8
50g/2oz/½ cup plain flour
15g/½oz/1 tbsp butter
1 egg plus 1 egg yolk
50g/2oz/1 cup finely grated mature
   Cheddar cheese
15ml/1 tbsp grated Parmesan cheese
2.5ml/½ tsp mustard powder
pinch of cayenne pepper
oil, for frying
salt and black pepper

1 Sift the flour on to a square of
greaseproof paper and set aside.
Place the butter and 150ml/¼ pint/
⅔ cup water in a pan and heat gently
until the butter has melted.

2 Bring the liquid to the boil and tip
in the flour all at once. Remove
from the heat and stir well with a
wooden spoon until the mixture begins
to leave the sides of the pan and forms
a ball. Allow to cool slightly.

3 Beat the egg and egg yolk together
in a bowl with a fork and then gradually add to the mixture in the pan,
beating well after each addition.

4 Stir the cheeses, mustard powder
and cayenne pepper into the
mixture and season well.

5 Heat the oil in a pan to 190°C/
375°F or until a cube of bread
browns in 30 seconds. Drop four
spoonfuls of the cheese mixture into
the oil at a time and deep-fry for 2–3
minutes until golden. Drain on kitchen
paper and keep hot in the oven while
cooking the remaining mixture. Serve
two puffs per person with a spoonful of
mango chutney and green salad.

Golden Parmesan Chicken

These chicken bites are equally good served cold with the garlicky mayonnaise.

INGREDIENTS

Serves 4

4 chicken breast fillets, skinned
75g/3oz/1½ cups fresh white
  breadcrumbs
40g/1½oz Parmesan cheese, finely
  grated
30ml/2 tbsp chopped fresh parsley
2 eggs, beaten
100ml/3½fl oz/½ cup good-quality
  mayonnaise
100ml/3½fl oz/½ cup fromage frais
1–2 garlic cloves, crushed
50g/2oz/4 tbsp butter, melted
salt and black pepper

1 Cut each chicken fillet into four or five large chunks. Mix together the breadcrumbs, Parmesan, parsley and seasoning in a shallow dish.

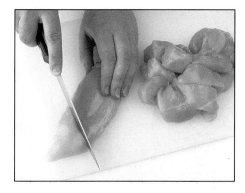

2 Dip the chicken pieces in the egg, then into the breadcrumb mixture. Place in a single layer on a baking sheet and chill for at least 30 minutes.

3 Meanwhile, to make the garlic mayonnaise, mix together the mayonnaise, fromage frais, garlic and pepper to taste. Spoon the mayonnaise into a small serving bowl. Chill until required.

4 Preheat the oven to 180°C/350°F/ Gas 4. Drizzle the melted butter over the chicken pieces and cook for about 20 minutes, until crisp and golden. Serve the chicken immediately with a crisp green salad and the garlic mayonnaise for dipping.

Pizzas & Pastries

Tartlets and turnovers make perfect party food any time of the year and on all sorts of occasions – try Tomato and Cheese Tarts or Leek and Broccoli Tartlets. Serve them hot or cold either to eat with a knife or fork, or as substantial finger food. Pizzas can be made any shape or size, and there are plenty of delicious fillings to tempt, try pepperoni, tuna and prawn, or mushroom and pancetta.

Pepperoni Pizza

INGREDIENTS

Makes a 30cm/12in pizza

For the sauce
30ml/2 tbsp olive oil
1 onion, finely chopped
1 garlic clove, crushed
400g/14oz can chopped tomatoes
 with herbs
15ml/1 tbsp tomato purée

For the pizza base
275g/10oz/2½ cups plain flour
2.5ml/½ tsp salt
5ml/1 tsp easy-blend yeast
30ml/2 tbsp olive oil

For the topping
½ red pepper, sliced into rings
½ yellow pepper, sliced into rings
½ green pepper, sliced into rings
150g/5oz mozzarella cheese, sliced
75g/3oz/½ cup pepperoni sausage,
 thinly sliced
8 black olives, stoned
3 sun-dried tomatoes, chopped
2.5ml/½ tsp dried oregano
olive oil, for drizzling

1 To make the sauce, heat the oil in a saucepan and add the onions and garlic. Fry gently for about 6–7 minutes, until softened. Add the tomatoes and stir in the tomato purée. Bring to the boil and boil rapidly for 5 minutes, until reduced slightly. Remove the pan from the heat and leave to cool.

2 For the pizza base, lightly grease a 30cm/12in round pizza tray. Sift the flour and salt into a bowl. Sprinkle over the easy-blend yeast and make a well in the centre. Pour in 175ml/ 6fl oz/¾ cup warm water and the olive oil. Mix to a soft dough.

3 Place the dough on a lightly floured surface and knead for about 5–10 minutes, until smooth. Roll out to a 25cm/10in round, making the edges slightly thicker than the centre. Lift the dough on to the pizza tray.

4 Spread the tomato sauce over the dough and then top with the peppers, mozzarella, pepperoni, black olives and tomatoes. Sprinkle over the oregano and drizzle with olive oil. Cover loosely and leave in a warm place for 30 minutes, until slightly risen. Meanwhile, preheat the oven to 220°C/425°F/Gas 7.

5 Bake for 25–30 minutes and serve hot straight from the tray.

Deep Pan Vegetable Pizza

INGREDIENTS

Serves 4

175g/6oz pizza dough (see Cook's Tip)
115g/4oz/½ cup canned creamed
  mushrooms
50g/2oz each cooked green beans,
  cauliflower florets, yellow pepper,
  seeded and chopped, and baby
  sweetcorn
6–8 tiny tomatoes, halved
2–3 pieces sun-dried tomato in oil
30ml/2 tbsp ready-made tomato pizza
  sauce
50g/2oz/½ cup grated blue Stilton
  cheese
little oil
salt and black pepper

1 Stretch out the pizza dough and use
to line an 18cm/7in deep pizza pan,
or a shallow loose-based cake tin.
Spread the pizza base with the creamed
mushrooms.

2 Arrange the cooked vegetables
neatly over the top and sprinkle
with seasoning. Add the halved tomatoes and the sun-dried tomato cut into
tiny pieces.

3 Drizzle the tomato sauce over the
top and sprinkle on the cheese.
Brush with oil where necessary and
sprinkle with the seasoning. Leave in a
warm place for the dough to rise up to
the top of the tin.

4 Meanwhile, preheat the oven to
220°C/425°F/Gas 7. Bake the pizza
for 15–20 minutes, until golden all
over, bubbling in the middle and
becoming quite crispy at the edges.

--- COOK'S TIP ---

To make a quick pizza dough, mix
together 175g/6oz/1½ cups plain flour,
5ml/1 tsp salt and half a sachet of easy-
blend yeast. Stir in 15ml/1 tbsp oil and up
to 120ml/4fl oz/½ cup tepid water. Mix to
a soft dough, then knead for about 5 minutes until smooth.

Tuna and Prawn Pizza

INGREDIENTS

Serves 4

225g/8oz/2 cups plain flour
5ml/1 tsp salt
½ sachet easy-blend yeast
15ml/1 tbsp olive oil

For the topping

75–90g/5–6 tbsp ready-made tomato
　pizza sauce
200g/7oz can tuna in brine, partly
　drained
115g/4oz cooked, peeled prawns
50g/2oz/4 tbsp grated Cheddar cheese
50g/2oz/4 tbsp diced mozzarella
　cheese
1 large garlic clove, crushed
15–30ml/1–2 tbsp olive oil
15ml/1 tbsp snipped fresh chives
15ml/1 tbsp chopped fresh parsley
salt and black pepper

1 To make the pizza dough, sift the flour into a bowl and stir in the salt and yeast. Then stir in the oil and up to 150ml/¼ pint/⅔ cup tepid water.

2 Gradually bring the dough together into a ball and knead for 5–10 minutes, until smooth and springy. Roll or stretch out to a 25cm/10in circle and place on a greased baking sheet.

3 Preheat the oven to 220°C/425°F/ Gas 7. Spread the tomato sauce over the base, then the tuna. Arrange the prawns on top and the two different cheeses.

4 Mix the garlic, oil, seasoning and herbs together and spoon all over the pizza. Leave the pizza to stand in a warm place for about 5 minutes, then cook for 15–20 minutes, until the base is crisp and the top melting.

—————— COOK'S TIP ——————

The basic pizza dough is suitable for all types of pizza and takes only minutes to mix together.

Turkey and Avocado Pitta Pizzas

INGREDIENTS

Serves 4

8 plum tomatoes, quartered
45–60ml/3–4 tbsp olive oil
1 large ripe avocado
8 small round pitta breads
6–7 slices cooked turkey, chopped
1 onion, very thinly sliced
275g/10oz/2½ cups grated sharp
  Cheddar cheese
30ml/2 tbsp chopped fresh coriander
salt and black pepper

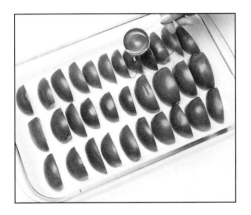

1 Preheat the oven to 230°C/450°F/ Gas 8. Place the tomatoes in a shallow ovenproof dish. Drizzle over 15ml/1 tbsp of the oil and season with salt and pepper. Bake for 30 minutes.

2 Mash the tomatoes with a fork, removing the skins as you mash. Set the tomatoes aside.

3 Halve, stone and peel the avocado, then cut into sixteen thin slices.

4 Brush the edges of the pitta breads with olive oil. Arrange the pitta breads on two baking sheets.

5 Spread each pitta with mashed tomato, almost to the edges.

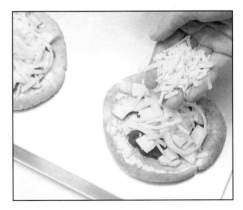

6 Top each with two avocado slices. Sprinkle with the turkey, then add a few onion slices and season with salt and pepper. Sprinkle on the cheese.

7 Bake the pitta pizzas for 15–20 minutes, until the cheese is golden. Sprinkle with the chopped coriander and serve hot.

Mushroom and Pancetta Pizzas

INGREDIENTS

Serves 4

For the base
225g/8oz/2 cups strong white flour
2.5ml/½ tsp salt
5ml/1 tsp easy-blend dried yeast
30ml/2 tbsp olive oil

For the topping
60ml/4 tbsp olive oil
2 garlic cloves, crushed
225g/8oz fresh ceps or chestnut
 mushrooms, roughly chopped
75g/3oz pancetta, roughly chopped
15ml/1 tbsp chopped fresh oregano
45ml/3 tbsp grated Parmesan cheese
salt and black pepper

1 To make the base, put the flour, salt and yeast into a food processor and process for a few seconds. Measure 150ml/¼ pint/⅔ cup warm water into a jug and add the olive oil. With the machine running, add the liquid until the mixture forms a soft dough.

2 Turn out the dough on to a lightly floured surface and knead until smooth and elastic. Place in an oiled bowl and cover with clear film. Leave the dough in a warm place for about 1 hour until doubled in size.

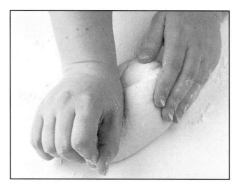

3 Turn out the dough on to a floured surface and divide into four pieces.

4 Roll out each piece of dough thinly to a 13cm/5in round. Place the pizza bases on a lightly greased baking sheet and set aside.

5 Preheat the oven to 220°C/425°F/ Gas 7. Heat 30ml/2 tbsp of the olive oil in a frying pan. Add the garlic and mushrooms and fry gently until the mushrooms are tender and the juices have evaporated. Season, then cool.

6 Brush the pizza bases with 15ml/ 1 tbsp oil, then spoon over the mushrooms. Scatter over the pancetta and oregano. Sprinkle with Parmesan and drizzle over the remaining oil. Bake for 10–15 minutes, until crisp.

COOK'S TIP

Look out for pancetta in major supermarkets and Italian delis. If you can't find it, thickly sliced bacon may be used instead.

Spiced Sweet Potato Turnovers

INGREDIENTS

Serves 4

For the filling
1 sweet potato, about 225g/8oz, scrubbed
30ml/2 tbsp vegetable oil
2 shallots, finely chopped
10ml/2 tsp coriander seeds, crushed
5ml/1 tsp ground cumin
5ml/1 tsp garam masala
115g/4oz frozen petit pois, cooked
15ml/1 tbsp chopped fresh mint
salt and black pepper
mint sprigs, to garnish

For the pastry
15ml/1 tbsp olive oil
1 size 5 egg
150ml/¼ pint/⅔ cup natural yogurt
115g/4oz/½ cup butter, melted
275g/10oz/2½ cups plain flour
1.25ml/¼ tsp bicarbonate of soda
5ml/1 tsp paprika
5ml/1 tsp salt
beaten egg, to glaze

1 Cook the sweet potato in boiling salted water for 15–20 minutes, until tender. Drain well and leave to cool. Peel the potato and cut the flesh into 1cm/½ in cubes.

2 Heat the oil in a frying pan and cook the shallots until softened. Add the sweet potato and fry until it browns at the edges. Add the spices and fry for a few seconds. Remove from the heat and add the peas, mint and seasoning to taste. Leave to cool.

3 Preheat the oven to 200°C/400°F/ Gas 6. To make the pastry, whisk the oil and egg in a bowl. Stir in the yogurt, then gradually add the melted butter until thoroughly blended.

4 Sift together the flour, bicarbonate of soda, paprika and salt into a bowl, then gradually stir into the yogurt mixture to form a soft dough. Knead and roll out the dough on a lightly floured surface, then stamp out rounds using a 10cm/4in cutter.

5 Spoon about 10ml/2 tsp of the filling on to one side of each round, then fold over and seal the edges. Re-roll the trimmings and stamp out more rounds until the filling is used up.

6 Arrange the turnovers on a greased baking sheet and brush with beaten egg. Bake for about 20 minutes, until crisp and golden brown. Serve hot, garnished with mint sprigs.

Curried Lamb Samosas

INGREDIENTS

Serves 4

15ml/1 tbsp oil
1 garlic clove, crushed
175g/6oz minced lamb
4 spring onions, finely chopped
10ml/2 tsp medium curry paste
4 ready-to-eat dried apricots, chopped
1 small potato, diced
10ml/2 tsp apricot chutney
30ml/2 tbsp frozen peas
a good squeeze of lemon juice
15ml/1 tbsp fresh chopped coriander
225g/8oz puff pastry
beaten egg, to glaze
5ml/1 tsp cumin seeds
salt and black pepper
45ml/3 tbsp natural yogurt and 15ml/
  1 tbsp chopped fresh mint, to serve
fresh mint sprigs, to garnish

1 Preheat the oven to 220°C/425°F/ Gas 7 and dampen a large, non-stick baking sheet.

2 Heat the oil in a frying pan and fry the garlic for 30 seconds, then add the minced lamb. Continue frying for about 5 minutes, stirring frequently until the meat is well browned.

3 Stir in the spring onions, curry paste, apricots and potato, and cook for 2–3 minutes. Add the apricot chutney, peas and 60ml/4 tbsp water. Cover and simmer for 10 minutes, stirring occasionally. Stir in the lemon juice and chopped coriander, season, remove from the heat and leave to cool.

4 On a floured surface, roll out the pastry and cut into four 15cm/6in squares. Place a quarter of the curry mixture in the centre of each pastry square and brush the edges with beaten egg. Fold over to make a triangle and seal the edges. Knock up the edges with the back of a knife and make a small slit in the top of each.

5 Brush each samosa with beaten egg and sprinkle over the cumin seeds. Place on the damp baking sheet and bake for 20 minutes. Serve with yogurt and mint and garnish with mint sprigs.

Leek and Stilton Samosas

Samosas make great party bites, especially if you prepare them well in advance and freeze them ready to cook. You could use another type of cheese such as Cheddar or mozzarella.

INGREDIENTS

Makes 16

2 leeks, sliced
30ml/2 tbsp milk
15ml/1 tbsp orange juice
75g/3oz/¾ cup Stilton cheese, crumbled
  or diced
8 sheets filo pastry
25g/1oz/2 tbsp butter, melted
black pepper

1 Very gently cook the leeks in the milk and orange juice for about 8–10 minutes until really soft, then season with pepper. Allow to cool slightly before mixing in the Stilton.

2 Lay out one sheet of pastry flat, brush it with butter and cut in half to make a long oblong strip. Place one-sixteenth of the leek and Stilton mixture in the bottom right hand corner. Fold the corner point up and over the filling towards the left edge to form a triangular shape.

3 Next, fold the bottom left hand point up to give a straight bottom edge to the pastry sheet, then fold the pastry triangle over to the right and then up again, so that the filling is completely enclosed.

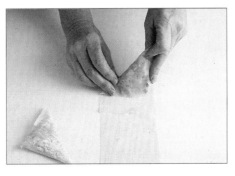

4 Preheat the oven to 200°C/400°F/ Gas 6. Continue folding up the sheet of pastry and tuck the top flap underneath. Brush with very little butter and place on a baking sheet.

5 Repeat this process for the rest of the pastry and filling mixture, to make about 16 samosas in all.

6 Bake the samosas for 10–15 minutes, until golden brown and crisp. Serve hot as a starter, or to pass round with drinks.

FREEZER NOTE

To freeze, stack the uncooked samosas between sheets of greaseproof paper and then wrap tightly in clear film. Freeze for up to 6 months. Defrost for 1 hour before cooking for 12–18 minutes, until hot and golden brown.

Salmon Filo Parcels

Serve these little savoury parcels just as they are for a party, or with a pool of fresh tomato sauce for a special starter.

INGREDIENTS 🍎

Makes 12
100g/3½oz can red or pink salmon
15ml/1 tbsp chopped fresh coriander
4 spring onions, finely chopped
4 sheets filo pastry
sunflower oil, for brushing
spring onions and lettuce, to serve

COOK'S TIP

When you are using filo pastry, it is important to prevent it drying out; cover any you are not using with a dish towel or clear film.

1 Preheat the oven to 200°C/400°F/ Gas 6. Lightly oil a baking sheet. Drain the salmon, discarding any skin and bones, then place in a bowl.

2 Flake the salmon with a fork and mix with the chopped fresh coriander and spring onions.

3 Place a single sheet of filo pastry on a work surface and brush lightly with oil. Place another sheet on top. Cut into six squares, each about 10cm/ 4in. Repeat with the remaining pastry, to make 12 squares.

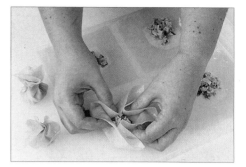

4 Place a spoonful of the salmon mixture on each square. Brush the edges of the pastry with oil, then draw together, pressing to seal. Place on a baking sheet and bake for 12–15 minutes, until golden. Serve warm, with spring onions and lettuce.

VARIATION

Use canned tuna fish or crabmeat in place of the pink or red salmon in these parcels, if you prefer.

Tomato and Cheese Tarts

These crisp little tartlets are easier to make than they look. Best eaten fresh from the oven.

INGREDIENTS 🍎

Serves 4
2 sheets filo pastry
1 egg white
115g/4oz low fat cream cheese
handful fresh basil leaves
3 small tomatoes, sliced
salt and black pepper

1 Preheat the oven to 200°C/400°F/ Gas 6. Brush the sheets of filo pastry lightly with egg white and cut into sixteen 10cm/ 4in squares.

2 Layer the squares in twos, in eight bun tins. Spoon the cheese into the pastry cases. Season with black pepper and top with basil leaves.

3 Arrange tomatoes on the tarts, add seasoning, and bake for 10–12 minutes, until golden. Serve warm.

COOK'S TIP

If you prefer, use tiny cherry tomatoes for these tarts – choose a mixture of red and yellow tomatoes if you can find them, then simply halve them and spoon into the tart cases.

Leek and Broccoli Tartlets

INGREDIENTS

Serves 4

175g/6oz/1½ cups plain flour, sifted
115g/4oz/½ cup butter
25g/1oz finely grated pecorino cheese
  or young, mild Parmesan
2 small leeks, sliced
75g/3oz tiny broccoli florets
150ml/¼ pint/⅔ cup milk
2 eggs
30ml/2 tbsp double cream
few pinches ground mace
salt and black pepper
15g/½oz flaked almonds, toasted, to
  garnish

1 Blend the flour, butter and cheese together in a food processor to give a fine crumb consistency. Add salt to taste. Stir in 60–90ml/4–6 tbsp cold water and bring the pastry together in a ball. Chill for 15 minutes.

2 Preheat the oven to 190°C/375°F/ Gas 5. Roll out the pastry on a floured surface and use to line four 10cm/4in tartlet tins. Line the pastry cases with greaseproof paper and fill with baking beans. Bake the pastry cases blind for 15 minutes, then remove the paper and cook for a further 5 minutes to dry out the bases.

3 To make the filling, place the vegetables in a pan and cook them in the milk for 2–3 minutes. Strain the milk into a small bowl and whisk in the eggs, mace, seasoning and cream.

4 Arrange the vegetables in the pastry cases and pour over the egg mixture. Bake for 20 minutes, or until the filling is just firm. Sprinkle with almonds before serving.

— COOK'S TIP —

Cook and freeze the tartlet cases, ready for easy weekend meals. They only need 15 minutes defrosting. Use other colourful, crunchy vegetables in season.

Crab and Ricotta Tartlets

Use the meat from a freshly cooked crab, weighing about 450g / 1 lb, if you can. Otherwise, look out for frozen brown and white crabmeat.

INGREDIENTS

Serves 4
225g/8oz/2 cups plain flour
pinch of salt
115g/4oz/½ cup butter, diced
225g/8oz/1 cup ricotta
15ml/1 tbsp grated onion
30ml/2 tbsp freshly grated Parmesan
  cheese
2.5ml/½ tsp mustard powder
2 eggs, plus 1 egg yolk
225g/8oz crabmeat
30ml/2 tbsp chopped fresh parsley
2.5–5ml/½–1 tsp anchovy essence
5–10ml/1–2 tsp lemon juice
salt and cayenne pepper
salad leaves, to garnish

1 Preheat the oven to 200°C/400°F/ Gas 6. Sift the flour and salt into a bowl, add the butter and rub it in until the mixture resembles fine bread-crumbs. Stir in about 60ml/4 tbsp cold water to make a firm dough.

2 Turn the dough on to a floured surface and knead lightly. Roll out the pastry and use to line four 10cm/4in tartlet tins. Prick the bases with a fork, then chill for 30 minutes.

3 Line the pastry cases with grease-proof paper and fill with baking beans. Bake for 10 minutes, then remove the paper and beans. Return to the oven and bake for a further 10 minutes.

4 Place the ricotta, grated onion, Parmesan and mustard powder in a bowl and beat until soft. Gradually beat in the eggs and egg yolk.

5 Gently stir in the crabmeat and chopped parsley, then add the anchovy essence, lemon juice, salt and cayenne pepper, to taste.

6 Remove the tartlet cases from the oven and reduce the temperature to 180°C/350°F/Gas 4. Spoon the filling into the cases and bake for 20 minutes, until set and golden brown. Serve hot with a garnish of salad leaves.

Cheese and Herb Turnovers

INGREDIENTS

Makes about 40

225g/8oz plain flour
1.5ml/¼ tsp grated nutmeg
2.5ml/½ tsp salt
150g/5oz cold butter or white cooking
 fat, or a combination of both
90–120ml/6–8 tbsp iced water

For the filling

2 eggs
115g/4oz grated mature Cheddar cheese
hot pepper sauce
15ml/1 tbsp finely chopped mixed
 fresh herbs, such as thyme, chives,
 and sage

1 To make the pastry, sift the flour, nutmeg, and salt into a bowl. Using a pastry blender or two knives, cut the butter or white cooking fat into the dry ingredients as quickly as possible until the mixture is crumbly and resembles breadcrumbs.

2 Sprinkle 90ml/6 tbsp of the iced water over the flour mixture. Combine with a fork until the dough holds together. If the dough is too crumbly, add a little more water, 15ml/1 tbsp at a time. Gather the dough into a ball.

3 Divide the dough in half and pat each portion into a round. Wrap the rounds in greaseproof paper and chill them for at least 20 minutes. Preheat the oven to 220°C/425°F/Gas 7.

4 To make the filling, put the eggs in a mixing bowl and beat well with a fork. Add the cheese, hot pepper sauce to taste, and the herbs.

5 On a lightly floured surface, roll out the dough to a thickness of 3mm/ ⅛in or less. Cut out rounds using a 7.5cm/3in cutter or drinking glass.

6 Place 5ml/1 tsp of filling in the centre of each pastry round. Fold over to make half-moon shapes, and press the edges together with the tines of a fork. A bit of filling may ooze through the seam.

7 Cut a few small slashes in the top of each pastry with the point of a sharp knife. Place on ungreased baking sheets. Bake until the pastries start to darken slightly, 18–20 minutes. To test for doneness, cut one in half; the pastry should be cooked through. Serve warm with drinks.

--- COOK'S TIP ---

The turnovers may be made ahead of time. Let them cool on a wire rack and then store in an airtight container. Just before serving, reheat the pastries in a preheated 190°C/375°F/Gas 5 oven for 5–10 minutes.

SNACKS & SANDWICHES

The recipes here will appeal to everyone with a hearty appetite. There are enticing 'sandwiches' – hot ones such as Tuna Croissants, and Tomato and Garlic Muffin Parcels, as well as delicious variations with cold fillings such as Chicken Pittas with Red Coleslaw, and Wholemeal SLTs. Or try potatoes, either baked in their jackets, or cooked as crisp skins to stuff or serve with a dip.

Cheese and Pepper Potato Skins

INGREDIENTS

Serves 6

3 baking potatoes, about 350g/12oz
  each, scrubbed and patted dry
15ml/1 tbsp vegetable oil
45ml/3 tbsp butter
1 onion, chopped
1 green pepper, seeded and
  coarsely chopped
15ml/1 tsp paprika
1 cup grated Cheddar cheese
salt and black pepper

1 Preheat the oven to 230°C/450°F/ Gas 8. Brush the potatoes all over with the oil. Prick them in several places on all sides with a fork.

3 Meanwhile, heat the butter in a large non-stick frying pan. Add the onion and a little salt and cook over a medium heat until softened, about 5 minutes. Add the pepper and continue cooking for 2–3 minutes more until just tender but still crunchy. Stir in the paprika and set aside.

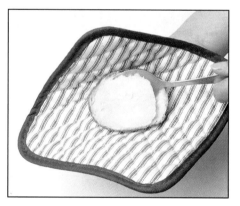

5 Add the potato flesh to the pan and cook over high heat, stirring, until the potato is lightly browned. Season with pepper.

6 Divide the vegetable mixture among the potato skins.

4 When the potatoes are cooked, halve them lengthways. Scoop out the flesh, keeping the pieces coarse. Keep the potato skins warm. Preheat the grill.

--- VARIATION ---

For Bacon Potato Skins, add 115g/4oz chopped cooked bacon to the cooked potato flesh and vegetables. Stuff as above.

7 Sprinkle the cheese on top. Grill for 3–5 minutes until the cheese just melts. Serve immediately.

2 Place the potatoes in a baking dish and bake for about 1½ hours until tender.

Tuna Chilli Tacos

Tacos are a useful, quick party snack – but you will need to use both hands to eat them!

INGREDIENTS

Makes 8

8 taco shells
400g/14oz can red kidney beans, drained
120ml/4fl oz/½ cup low fat fromage frais
2.5ml/½ tsp chilli sauce
2 spring onions, chopped
5ml/1 tsp chopped fresh mint
½ small crisp lettuce, shredded
425g/15oz can tuna chunks in water, drained
50g/2oz/¾ cup grated reduced-fat Cheddar cheese
8 cherry tomatoes, quartered
mint sprigs, to garnish

1 Warm the taco shells in a hot oven for a few minutes until crisp.

2 Mash the beans lightly with a fork, then stir in the fromage frais, chilli sauce, spring onions, and mint.

3 Fill the taco shells with the shredded lettuce, the bean mixture, and tuna. Top the filled shells with the cheese and serve at once with the tomatoes, garnished with sprigs of mint.

VARIATION

This tuna chilli mixture would make an excellent filling for crisp, grilled potato skins, too (see below).

Potato Skins with Cajun Dip

No need to deep-fry potato skins for this treat – grilling crisps them up in no time.

INGREDIENTS

Serves 2

2 large baking potatoes
120ml/4fl oz/½ cup natural yogurt
1 garlic clove, crushed
5ml/1 tsp tomato paste
2.5ml/½ tsp green chilli paste (or ½ small green chilli, chopped
1.5ml/¼ tsp celery salt
salt and black pepper

1 Bake or microwave the potatoes until tender. Cut them in half and scoop out the flesh, leaving a thin layer on the skins. Keep the scooped out potato for another meal.

2 Cut each potato in half again then place the pieces skin-side down on a large baking sheet.

3 Grill for 4–5 minutes, or until crisp. Mix together the dip ingredients and serve with the potato skins.

COOK'S TIP

If you don't have any chilli paste or fresh chillies, then add a drop or two of hot pepper sauce to the dip instead.

Chicken Pittas with Red Coleslaw

Pittas are great for a teenage party, just supply the ingredients and let the party-goers assemble the pittas as they eat!

INGREDIENTS 🍎

Serves 4

¼ red cabbage, finely shredded
1 small red onion, finely sliced
2 radishes, thinly sliced
1 red apple, peeled, cored, and grated
15ml/1 tbsp lemon juice
45ml/3 tbsp low fat fromage frais
1 cooked chicken breast without skin, about 175g/6oz
4 large pittas or 8 small pittas
salt and black pepper
chopped fresh parsley, to garnish

1 Remove the tough central spine from the cabbage leaves, then finely shred the leaves using a large sharp knife. Place the shredded cabbage in a bowl and stir in the onion, radishes, apple, and lemon juice.

2 Stir the fromage frais into the shredded cabbage mixture and season well with salt and pepper. Thinly slice the cooked chicken breast and stir into the shredded cabbage mixture until well coated in fromage frais.

3 Toast the pittas until warmed, then split them along one edge using a round-bladed knife. Spoon the filling into the pittas, then garnish with chopped fresh parsley.

--- COOK'S TIP ---

If the filled pittas need to be made more than an hour in advance, line the pitta breads with crisp lettuce leaves before adding the filling.

Wholemeal SLTs

A quick, tasty snack for children's parties packed with a healthy combination – sardines, lettuce, and tomatoes!

INGREDIENTS 🍎

Serves 2

2 small wholemeal rolls
130g/4¼oz can sardines in olive oil
4 crisp green lettuce leaves, such as
   escarole
1 beefsteak tomato, sliced
juice of ½ lemon
salt and black pepper

1 Slice the rolls in half crossways using a sharp knife. Drain off the oil from the sardines into a small bowl, then brush the cut surfaces of the rolls with a small amount of the oil.

2 Cut or break the sardines into small pieces, then fill each roll with a lettuce leaf, some sliced tomato, and pieces of sardine, sprinkling the filling with a little lemon juice, and salt and pepper to taste.

3 Sandwich the rolls back together and press the lids down lightly with your hand. Serve at once.

--- VARIATION ---

As an alternative, replace the sardines with tuna packed in oil, or try mackerel fillets in oil and be generous with the black pepper.

--- COOK'S TIP ---

Don't make these filled rolls until you are almost ready to serve them, or they may become soggy.

Spicy Baked Potatoes

INGREDIENTS 🍎

Serves 2–4

2 large baking potatoes
5ml/1 tsp sunflower oil
1 small onion, finely chopped
2.5cm/1in piece fresh root ginger, grated
5ml/1 tsp ground cumin
5ml/1 tsp ground coriander
2.5ml/½ tsp ground turmeric
garlic salt
natural yogurt and fresh coriander
  sprigs, to serve

1 Preheat the oven to 190°C/375°F/ Gas 5. Prick the potatoes with a fork. Bake for 40 minutes, or until soft.

2 Cut the potatoes in half and scoop out the flesh. Heat the oil in a non-stick pan and sauté the onion for a few minutes to soften. Stir in the ginger, cumin, coriander, and turmeric.

3 Stir over a low heat for about 2 minutes, then add the potato flesh and garlic salt to taste.

4 Cook the potato mixture for 2 minutes more, stirring occasionally. Spoon the mixture back into the potato shells and top each with a spoonful of natural yogurt and a sprig or two of fresh coriander. Serve hot.

— COOK'S TIP —
If you don't have all the individual ground spices, you could use 10–15ml/2–3 tsp curry powder or paste instead.

Two Beans Provençal

INGREDIENTS 🍎

Serves 4

5ml/1 tsp olive oil
1 small onion, finely chopped
1 garlic clove, crushed
225g/8oz French beans
225g/8oz runner beans
2 tomatoes, peeled and chopped
salt and black pepper

— COOK'S TIP —
To peel tomatoes, dip them into boiling water for 30 seconds, then rinse in cold water – the skins should simply peel off.

1 Heat the oil in a heavy-based, or non-stick, pan and sauté the chopped onion over medium heat until softened but not browned.

2 Add the garlic, both the beans, and the tomatoes, then season well and cover tightly.

3 Cook over a fairly low heat, shaking the pan occasionally, for about 30 minutes, or until the beans are tender. Serve hot.

Tomato and Garlic Muffin Parcels

INGREDIENTS

Serves 4

4 muffins
25g/1oz/2 tbsp garlic butter, softened
2 medium tomatoes
8 small pieces mozzarella or Edam
  cheese
salt and black pepper

1 Preheat the oven to 190°C/375°F/
Gas 5. Cut the muffins almost, but
not completely, in halves horizontally.

2 Spread each half with a little garlic
butter. Slice the tomatoes and
arrange on the bases, then sprinkle with
seasoning to taste.

3 Slide the slices of mozzarella or
Edam cheese on top of the tomatoes, then close the muffins neatly and
wrap in foil. Put the parcels on a baking sheet and bake for 20 minutes.

4 Serve the muffins hot with a selection of tangy chutneys and pickles,
if you like.

FREEZER NOTE

Prepare the filled muffins and freeze them,
wrapped, ready to heat through from
frozen.

Tuna Croissants

These unusual sandwiches are perfect for informal gatherings – serve
them cold or warm them through
in the oven to serve immediately.

INGREDIENTS

Serves 4

4 large fresh croissants
175g/6oz can tuna and sweetcorn in
  mayonnaise dressing
8 crisp lettuce leaves
2 tomatoes, sliced
30ml/2 tbsp chopped green olives
salt and black pepper

1 Split the croissants in half horizontally and then warm them through
in the oven, if you wish.

2 Place the tuna and sweetcorn in a
small bowl and mix well. Tear the
lettuce into large pieces and arrange on
the bottom halves of the croissants,
then add the tomato slices.

3 Spoon the tuna and sweetcorn
mixture over the tomatoes and scatter over the olives. Sprinkle with
seasoning to taste, then replace the
croissant tops and serve at once.

COOK'S TIP

Use chopped boiled eggs, peeled prawns,
cooked chicken or bacon, mixed with a
little mayonnaise, in place of the tuna, if
you like.

Lemon and Herb Risotto Wedges

This unusual rice dish makes a substantial party snack. Serve hot on plates, or cut into thin wedges and serve cold as finger food.

INGREDIENTS 🍎

Serves 4

1 small leek, thinly sliced
600ml/1 pint/2½ cups chicken stock
225g/8oz/1 cup short grain rice
finely grated rind of 1 lemon
30ml/2 tbsp chopped fresh chives
30ml/2 tbsp chopped fresh parsley
75g/3oz/¾ cup shredded mozzarella cheese
salt and black pepper
parsley and lemon wedges, to garnish

1 Preheat the oven to 200°C/400°F/Gas 6. Lightly oil a deep-sided 22cm/8½ in round, loose-bottomed cake pan.

2 Cook the leek in a large pan with 45ml/3 tbsp of the stock, stirring over a moderate heat, to soften. Add the rice and the remaining stock.

3 Bring to the boil. Cover the pan and simmer gently, stirring occasionally, for about 20 minutes, or until all the liquid is absorbed.

4 Stir in the lemon rind, herbs, cheese, and seasoning. Spoon into the cake pan, cover with foil and bake for 30–35 minutes or until lightly browned. Turn out and serve in slices, garnished with parsley and lemon wedges.

COOK'S TIP

The best rice to choose for this recipe is the Italian round grain arborio rice, which should not be rinsed before use.

Tex-Mex Baked Potatoes with Chilli

INGREDIENTS

Serves 4

2 large potatoes
15ml/1 tbsp oil
1 garlic clove, crushed
1 small onion, chopped
½ small red pepper, seeded and chopped
225g/8oz lean minced beef
½ small fresh red chilli, seeded and
  chopped
5ml/1 tsp ground cumin
pinch of cayenne pepper
200g/7oz can chopped tomatoes
30ml/2 tbsp tomato purée
2.5ml/½ tsp dried oregano
2.5ml/½ tsp dried marjoram
200g/7oz can red kidney beans, drained
15ml/1 tbsp chopped fresh coriander
salt and black pepper
60ml/4 tbsp soured cream
chopped fresh parsley, to garnish

1 Preheat the oven to 220°C/425°F/ Gas 7. Rub the potatoes with a little oil and pierce with skewers. Bake them on the top shelf for 30 minutes before beginning to cook the chilli.

2 Heat the oil in a pan and add the garlic, onion and pepper. Fry gently for 4–5 minutes, until softened.

3 Add the beef and fry until browned all over, then stir in the chilli, cumin, cayenne pepper, tomatoes, tomato purée, 60ml/4 tbsp water and the herbs. Cover and simmer for about 25 minutes, stirring occasionally.

4 Remove the lid, stir in the kidney beans and cook for 5 minutes. Turn off the heat and stir in the chopped coriander. Season well and set aside.

5 Cut the baked potatoes in half and place them in serving bowls. Top with the chilli mixture and a dollop of soured cream and garnish with chopped fresh parsley.

Scrambled Egg and Salmon Muffins

This traditional British breakfast dish is delicious when piled high on top of a hot toasted wholemeal muffin for a substantial party snack.

INGREDIENTS

Serves 4

4 eggs
45ml/3 tbsp single cream or top of the milk
4 wholemeal muffins
25g/1oz/2 tbsp butter, plus extra for spreading
15ml/1 tbsp snipped chives
2.5ml/½ tsp grated lemon rind
115g/4oz smoked salmon or trout, snipped into strips
salt and black pepper
snipped chives, to garnish

1 Break the eggs into a bowl, pour on the cream or milk and season well. Beat lightly with a fork.

2 Halve the muffins and grill until lightly toasted on both sides. Spread with a little butter and keep warm.

3 Meanwhile, melt the butter in a saucepan over a gentle heat, add the eggs and stir occasionally with a wooden spoon until just beginning to set.

4 Add the chives, lemon rind and smoked salmon or trout and stir until just set but still moist. Spoon on to the toasted muffins and garnish with snipped chives. Serve at once.

—————— COOK'S TIP ——————

Don't overcook the scrambled eggs – remove the pan from the heat while they are still quite creamy.

Spanish Omelette

A traditional Spanish omelette consists of potato, onion and egg and is served as *tapas* or bar food. With mixed peppers and spicy sausage, it makes a filling party snack.

INGREDIENTS

Serves 4

60ml/4 tbsp olive oil
1 small onion, thinly sliced
1 small red pepper, seeded and sliced
1 small yellow pepper, seeded and sliced
1 large potato, peeled, boiled and diced
115g/4oz/1 cup sliced Chorizo sausage
4 eggs
salt and black pepper
chopped fresh parsley, to garnish

1 Heat 30ml/2 tbsp of the oil in a frying pan, add the onion and peppers and cook for 7 minutes, stirring occasionally until softened.

2 Add the remaining oil, potatoes and sausage and cook for a further 3–4 minutes. Reduce the heat slightly.

3 Place the eggs in a bowl, season well and beat lightly with a fork. Pour the eggs over the vegetable and sausage mixture and shake the pan gently.

4 Cook gently for about 5–6 minutes, until beginning to set. Place an upturned plate on top of the pan and carefully turn the omelette upside-down on to the plate.

5 Slide the omelette back into the pan and continue cooking for a further 3 minutes, until the centre is just set but still moist. Sprinkle with parsley, cut into wedges and serve straight from the pan.

Fried Cheese Triangles

Although very simple – or perhaps because of its simplicity – this quick snack has been popular for generations, and is enjoyed by all age groups.

INGREDIENTS

Serves 2–4

3 eggs
75ml/5 tbsp milk
45ml/3 tbsp chopped fresh herbs such
   as tarragon, parsley and chervil
4 slices bread
4 slices Red Leicester cheese
40g/1½oz/3 tbsp butter
salt and pepper

1 Lightly beat the eggs, milk, herbs and seasoning together. Pour into a large shallow dish.

2 Cut the crusts from the bread and make into sandwiches with the cheese. Cut them in half to make triangles, then dip both sides of each sandwich in the milk mixture.

3 Heat the butter in a frying pan, add the bread and fry until golden on both sides. Serve at once.

Savoury Scrambled Egg Fingers

Known as 'Scotch Woodcock', this dish was popular in Victorian and Edwardian times as a savoury served instead of cheese at the end of a meal – it makes a really tasty party nibble.

INGREDIENTS

Serves 2

2 slices bread
40g/1½oz/3 tbsp butter, plus extra for
   spreading
anchovy paste such as Gentleman's
   Relish
2 eggs, beaten
2 egg yolks
60–90ml/4–6 tbsp cream or milk
salt and pepper
anchovy fillets cut into strips, and
   paprika for garnish

1 Toast the bread, spread with butter and anchovy paste, then remove the crusts and cut into fingers. Keep warm, while you make the scrambled eggs.

2 Melt the rest of the butter in a non-stick saucepan, then stir in the eggs, egg yolks, cream or milk, a little salt, and pepper. Heat very gently, stirring constantly, until the mixture begins to thicken.

3 Remove the pan from the heat and continue to stir until the mixture becomes creamy.

4 Spoon the egg mixture evenly on to the toast fingers and garnish with strips of anchovy fillet and a sprinkling of paprika. Serve immediately.

SIMPLE SALADS

Whatever the season, salads make wonderful party dishes. Some, like Salade Niçoise, or Mexican Mixed Salad can be served as a main course, while others make ideal accompaniments to all sorts of foods. Choose the salad according to what is available – crisp leaves with fruit or herbs are perfect in the summer months, while colourful vegetable combinations work well in the cooler seasons.

Salade Niçoise

INGREDIENTS

Serves 4

90ml/6 tbsp olive oil
30ml/2 tbsp tarragon vinegar
5ml/1 tsp tarragon or Dijon mustard
1 small garlic clove, crushed
115g/4oz/1 cup French beans
12 small new or salad potatoes
3–4 Little Gem lettuces, roughly
  chopped
200g/7oz can tuna in oil, drained
6 anchovy fillets, halved lengthways
12 black olives, stoned
4 tomatoes, chopped
4 spring onions, finely chopped
10ml/2 tsp capers
30ml/2 tbsp pine nuts
2 hard-boiled eggs, chopped
salt and black pepper
crusty bread, to serve

1 Mix the oil, vinegar, mustard, garlic and seasoning with a wooden spoon in the base of a large salad bowl.

2 Cook the French beans and potatoes in separate pans of boiling salted water until just tender. Drain and add to the bowl with the lettuce, tuna, anchovies, olives, tomatoes, spring onions and capers.

3 Just before serving toast the pine nuts in a small frying pan until lightly browned.

4 Sprinkle over the salad while still hot, add the eggs and toss all the ingredients together well. Serve with chunks of hot crusty bread.

--- COOK'S TIP ---

Look out for waxy salad potatoes like Charlotte, Belle de Fontenay or Pink Fir Apple – or simply use new season Jersey Royals.

Caesar Salad

For this famous salad, created by the Tijuanan chef called Caesar Cardini in the 1920s, the dressing is traditionally tossed into crunchy Cos lettuce, but any crisp lettuce will do.

INGREDIENTS

Serves 4

1 large cos lettuce
4 thick slices white or Granary bread
    without crusts, cubed
45ml/3 tbsp olive oil
1 garlic clove, crushed

For the dressing

1 egg
1 garlic clove, chopped
30ml/2 tbsp lemon juice
dash of Worcestershire sauce
3 anchovy fillets, chopped
120ml/4fl oz/½ cup olive oil
25g/1oz/5 tbsp grated Parmesan
    cheese
salt and black pepper

1 Preheat the oven to 220°C/425°F/ Gas 7. Separate, rinse and dry the lettuce leaves. Tear the outer leaves roughly and chop the heart. Arrange the lettuce in a large salad bowl.

2 Mix together the cubed bread, olive oil and garlic in a separate bowl until the bread has soaked up the oil. Lay the bread cubes on a baking sheet and place in the oven for about 6–8 minutes (keeping an eye on them) until golden. Remove and leave to cool.

3 To make the dressing, break the egg into the bowl of a food processor or blender and add the garlic, lemon juice, Worcestershire sauce and one of the anchovy fillets. Blend until smooth.

4 With the motor running, pour in the olive oil in a thin stream until the dressing has the consistency of single cream. Season with black pepper and a little salt if needed.

5 Pour the dressing over the salad leaves and toss well, then toss in the garlic croûtons, Parmesan cheese and the remaining anchovies and serve.

Mexican Mixed Salad

INGREDIENTS

Serves 4

10ml/2 tsp vegetable oil
450g/1lb lean minced beef
1 small onion, chopped
1.25ml/¼ tsp cayenne pepper, or to
  taste
200g/7oz can sweetcorn, drained
425g/15oz can kidney beans, drained
15ml/1 tbsp chopped fresh coriander,
  plus extra coriander leaves, to garnish
1 small Cos lettuce
3 tomatoes, sliced
225g/8oz/2 cups grated Cheddar
  cheese
1 avocado
50g/2oz stoned black olives, sliced
4 spring onions, chopped
salt and black pepper
tortilla chips, to serve

For the dressing

45ml/3 tbsp white wine vinegar
5ml/1 tsp Dijon mustard
30ml/2 tbsp single cream
150ml/¼ pint/⅔ cup vegetable oil
1 small garlic clove, finely chopped
5ml/1 tsp ground cumin
5ml/1 tsp dried oregano
salt and black pepper

─────── VARIATIONS ───────

For Chicken and Taco Salad, substitute
1lb boneless, skinless chicken breast, finely
diced, for the minced beef. Chick-peas
may be used in place of kidney beans.
Although frozen or canned sweetcorn is
convenient, freshly cooked sweetcorn ker-
nels scraped from the cob give added
moisture and extra flavour.

1 To make the dressing, mix the
vinegar and salt with a fork until
dissolved. Stir in the mustard and
cream. Gradually stir in the oil until
blended, then add the garlic, cumin,
oregano and pepper and set aside.

2 Heat the oil in a large frying pan.
Add the beef, onion, salt and
cayenne and cook for 5–7 minutes, until
just browned. Stir frequently to break
up any lumps. Drain and leave to cool.

3 Place the beef mixture, sweetcorn,
kidney beans and chopped coriander in a large bowl and toss to blend.

4 Stack the lettuce leaves on top of
one another and slice thinly,
crossways, into shreds. Place in another
bowl and toss with 45ml/3 tbsp of the
prepared dressing. Divide the lettuce
among four serving plates.

5 Mound the meat mixture in the
centre of the lettuce. Arrange the
tomatoes at the edge and sprinkle with
the grated cheese.

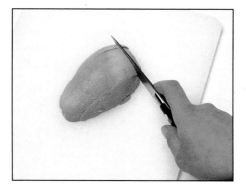

6 Halve, stone, peel and dice the
avocado and add to salad. Scatter
the olives and spring onions on top.
Pour the remaining dressing over the
salads and garnish with coriander.
Serve with tortilla chips.

New Potato and Chive Salad

The secret of a good potato salad is to mix the potatoes with the dressing while they are still hot so that they absorb it.

INGREDIENTS

Serves 4–6
675g/1½lb new potatoes (unpeeled)
4 spring onions
45ml/3 tbsp olive oil
15ml/1 tbsp white wine vinegar
3.75ml/¾ tsp Dijon mustard
175ml/6fl oz/¾ cup mayonnaise
45ml/3 tbsp snipped fresh chives
salt and pepper

1 Cook the potatoes in boiling salted water until tender. Meanwhile, finely chop the white parts of the spring onions along with a little of the green part.

2 Whisk together the oil, vinegar and mustard. Drain the potatoes well, then immediately toss lightly with the vinegar mixture and spring onions and leave to cool.

3 Stir the mayonnaise and chives into the potatoes and chill well until ready to serve with grilled sausages, chicken wings or cold meats.

—— COOK'S TIP ——

Look out for the small, waxy potatoes, sold especially for salads and cold dishes – they are particularly good in this recipe.

Lettuce and Herb Salad

Shops now sell many different types of lettuce leaves all year, so try to use a mixture. Look out for pre-packed bags of mixed baby lettuce leaves.

INGREDIENTS

Serves 4

½ cucumber
mixed lettuce leaves
1 bunch watercress, about 115g/4oz
1 chicory head, sliced
45ml/3 tbsp mixed chopped fresh herbs such as parsley, thyme, tarragon, chives and chervil

For the dressing

15ml/1 tbsp white wine vinegar
5ml/1 tsp mustard
75ml/5 tbsp olive oil
salt and black pepper

1 To make the dressing, mix the vinegar and mustard together, then whisk in the oil and seasoning.

2 Peel the cucumber, if liked, then halve the cucumber lengthways and scoop out the seeds. Thinly slice the flesh. Tear the lettuce leaves into bite-sized pieces.

3 Either toss the cucumber, lettuce, watercress, chicory and herbs together in a bowl, or arrange them in the bowl in layers.

4 Stir the dressing, then pour over the salad, toss lightly to coat the salad vegetables and leaves. Serve at once.

--- COOK'S TIP ---

Do not dress the salad until just before serving otherwise the lettuce leaves will wilt.

Quick Ratatouille Salad

Similar but different, quick but delicious is this salad. The key thing is that it keeps well, in fact, it improves if eaten the next day.

INGREDIENTS

Serves 4

1 small aubergine, about 225g/8oz
salt
60ml/4 tbsp olive oil
1 onion, sliced
1 green pepper, seeded and cut in strips
3 garlic cloves, crushed
15–30ml/1–2 tbsp cider vinegar
8 tiny firm tomatoes, halved
salt and mixed ground peppercorns
sprigs of oregano, to garnish

1 Slice and quarter the aubergine. Place in a colander and sprinkle with plenty of salt. Leave for 20 minutes and then drain off any liquid and rinse well under cold water.

2 Heat the oil in a large pan and gently sauté the onion, pepper and garlic, then stir in the aubergine and toss over a high heat for 5 minutes.

3 When the aubergine is beginning to turn golden, add the cider vinegar, tomatoes and seasoning to taste. Leave to cool, then chill well. Season to taste again before serving, garnished with sprigs of oregano.

— COOK'S TIP —

Once the aubergines are rinsed, squeeze them dry between sheets of kitchen paper – the drier they are, the quicker they will cook and brown.

Crisp Fruity Salad

Crisp lettuce, tangy cheese and crunchy pieces of fruit make a refreshing salad for any occasion.

INGREDIENTS

Serves 4

½ Webb's lettuce
75g/3oz grapes, seeded and halved
50g/2oz/½ cup mature Cheddar cheese, grated
1 large eating apple, cored and thinly sliced
90–105ml/6–7 tbsp mild French vinaigrette (see Cook's Tip)
45ml/3 tbsp garlic croûtons

1 Tear the lettuce leaves into small pieces and place in a salad bowl. Add the grapes, cheese and apples.

2 Pour the dressing over the salad. Mix well and serve at once, sprinkled with garlic croûtons.

— COOK'S TIP —

To make a light vinaigrette, mix 15ml/1 tbsp French mustard, 15ml/1 tbsp white wine vinegar, a pinch of sugar, and seasoning with 60ml/4tbsp sunflower oil.

Beetroot, Chicory and Orange Salad

A refreshing salad that goes well with grilled meats or fish. Alternatively, arrange it prettily on individual plates and serve as a summer starter.

INGREDIENTS ✿

Serves 4

2 medium cooked beetroot, diced
2 chicory heads, sliced
1 large orange
60ml/4 tbsp natural low fat yogurt
10ml/2 tsp wholegrain mustard
salt and black pepper

1 Mix together the diced, cooked beetroot and sliced chicory in a large serving bowl.

2 Finely grate the rind from the orange. With a sharp knife, remove all the peel and white pith. Cut out the segments, catching the juice in a bowl. Add the segments to the salad.

3 Add the orange rind, yogurt, mustard, and seasonings to the orange juice, mix thoroughly, then spoon over the salad.

VARIATION

If you prefer, use a selection of leaves instead of just chicory. Choose slightly bitter leaves such as curly endive, along with strongly flavoured leaves like rocket or spinach. Tear the leaves into pieces before mixing with the beetroot.

Roasted Pepper Salad

This colourful salad is very easy and can be made up to a day in advance, as the sharp-sweet dressing mingles with the mild pepper flavours.

INGREDIENTS ✿

Serves 4

3 large red, green and yellow peppers, halved and seeded
115g/4oz feta cheese, diced or crumbled
15ml/1 tbsp sherry vinegar or red wine vinegar
15ml/1 tbsp clear honey
salt and black pepper

1 Arrange the pepper halves in a single layer, skin side up, on a baking sheet. Place the peppers under a hot grill until the skin is blackened and beginning to blister.

2 Lift the peppers into a plastic bag and close the end. Leave until cool, then peel off and discard the skin.

3 Arrange the peppers on a platter and scatter over the cheese. Mix together the vinegar, honey, and seasonings, then sprinkle over the salad. Chill until ready to serve.

COOK'S TIP

This salad can be made up to one day in advance, if you like. Cover the dish tightly with an airtight lid or clear film and chill until ready to serve.

INDEX

Anchovy: Caesar salad, 87
  Salade Niçoise, 86
  savoury scrambled egg fingers, 82
Apples: crisp fruity salad, 92
Aubergines: aubergine sunflower pâté, 12
  quick ratatouille salad, 92
Avocados: chicken and avocado
    mayonnaise, 26
  Mexican dip with chilli chips, 15
  tangy avocado dip, 18
  turkey and avocado pitta pizzas, 55

Bacon: chicken, bacon and walnut
    terrine, 22
  spinach stuffed mushrooms, 41
  sweetcorn and bacon fritters, 36
Beans: Mexican mixed salad, 88
  Salade Niçoise, 86
  Tex-Mex baked potatoes with chilli, 79
  tuna chilli tacos, 70
  two beans Provençal, 74
Beef: Mexican mixed salad, 88
  Tex-Mex baked potatoes with chilli, 79
Beetroot, chicory and orange salad, 94
Blinis with smoked salmon and dill
    cream, 23
Bread: fried cheese triangles, 82
  Mediterranean garlic toast, 32
  mushroom croustades, 30
  pork and prawn toasts, 32
  tomato and pesto toasties, 31
  wholemeal SLTs, 73
Broccoli: leek and broccoli tartlets, 62
  Bruschetta, 32

Cabbage: chicken pittas with red coleslaw, 72
Caesar salad, 87
Celeriac fritters with mustard dip, 14
Celery: celery stuffed with Gorgonzola, 16
  nut and cheese stuffed celery sticks, 24
Cheese: Caesar salad, 87
  celery stuffed with Gorgonzola, 16
  cheese and herb turnovers, 64
  cheese and pepper potato skins, 68
  chicory with cheese and peppers, 26
  crab and ricotta tartlets, 63
  crisp fruity salad, 92
  crostini with cheese, 34
  fried cheese triangles, 82
  goat's cheese dip with herbs, 18
  golden cheese puffs, 48
  golden Parmesan chicken, 49
  leek and Stilton samosas, 59
  Mediterranean garlic toast, 32
  Mexican mixed salad, 88
  nut and cheese stuffed celery sticks, 24
  Parmesan fish goujons, 47
  ploughman's pâté, 21
  rice and cheese croquettes, 37
  roasted pepper salad, 94
  spinach stuffed mushrooms, 41
  tomato and garlic muffin parcels, 76
  tomato and cheese tarts, 60
Chicken: chicken and avocado
    mayonnaise, 26
  chicken and taco salad, 88
  chicken, bacon and walnut terrine, 22

Chinese chicken wings, 40
  chicken pittas with red coleslaw, 72
  golden Parmesan chicken, 49
  Chicken liver pâté with Marsala, 20
Chicory: beetroot, chicory and
    orange salad, 94
  chicory with cheese and peppers, 26
Chilli: garlic chilli prawns, 38
  Mexican dip with chilli chips, 15'
  potato skins with Cajun dip, 70
  Tex-Mex baked potatoes with chilli, 79
  tuna chilli tacos, 70
Chinese chicken wings, 40
Chives: new potato and chive salad, 90
Cod: Parmesan fish goujons, 47
  salmon and prawn fritters, 44
Coleslaw: chicken pittas with red
    coleslaw, 72
Crab and ricotta tartlets, 63
Croissants: tuna croissants, 76
Crostini: crostini with cheese, 34
  crostini with mussels, 35
Curry: curried lamb samosas, 58

Dill: blinis with smoked salmon and dill
    cream, 23
Dips: celeriac fritters with mustard dip, 14
  goat's cheese dip with herbs, 18
  Mexican dip with chilli chips, 15
  pepper dips with crudités, 12
  potato skins with Cajun dip, 70
  raw vegetables with olive oil dip, 16
  tangy avocado dip, 18

Eggs: fried cheese triangles, 82
  Salade Niçoise, 86
  savoury scrambled egg fingers, 82
  scrambled egg and salmon muffins, 80
  Spanish omelette, 80
  stuffed devilled eggs, 24

Filo pastry: leek and Stilton samosas, 59
  salmon filo parcels, 60
French beans: Salade Niçoise, 86
Fried fish goujons, 38

Garlic: garlic chilli prawns, 38
  Mediterranean garlic toast, 32
  tomato and garlic muffin parcels, 76
Golden cheese puffs, 48
Golden Parmesan chicken, 49
Goujons: fried fish goujons, 38
  Parmesan fish goujons, 47
Grapes: crisp fruity salad, 92

Haddock: Parmesan fish goujons, 47
  salmon and prawn fritters, 44
Ham: stuffed devilled eggs, 24
Herbs: blinis with smoked salmon and
    dill cream, 23
  cheese and herb turnovers, 64
  goat's cheese dip with herbs, 18
  lemon and herb risotto wedges, 78
  lettuce and herb salad, 91
  new potato and chive salad, 90

Kidney beans: Mexican mixed salad, 88

Tex-Mex baked potatoes with chilli, 79
  tuna chilli tacos, 70

Lamb: curried lamb samosas, 58
Leeks: leek and broccoli tartlets, 62
  leek and Stilton samosas, 59
Lemon and herb risotto wedges, 78
Lettuce: Caesar salad, 87
  crisp fruity salad, 92
  lettuce and herb salad, 91
  Mexican mixed salad, 88
  Salade Niçoise, 86
  wholemeal SLTs, 73

Mango: nut patties with mango relish, 46
Mediterranean garlic toast, 32
Mexican dip with chilli chips, 15
Mexican mixed salad, 88
Muffins: scrambled egg and salmon
    muffins, 80
  tomato and garlic muffin parcels, 76
Mushrooms: deep pan vegetable pizza, 53
  mushroom and pancetta pizzas, 56
  mushroom croustades, 30
  mushroom popovers, 42
  spinach stuffed mushrooms, 41
Mussels: crostini with mussels, 35
Mustard: celeriac fritters with mustard
    dip, 14

Nuts: nut patties with mango relish, 46

Olive oil: raw vegetables with olive oil
    dip, 16
Oranges: beetroot, chicory and
    orange salad, 94

Pancetta: mushroom and pancetta
    pizzas, 56
Pâtés and terrines: aubergine sunflower
    pâté, 12
  chicken liver pâté with Marsala, 20
  chicken, bacon and walnut terrine, 22
  Ploughman's pâté, 21
Pepperoni pizza, 52
Peppers: cheese and pepper potato
    skins, 68
  chicory with cheese and peppers, 26
  pepper dips with crudités, 12
  quick ratatouille salad, 92
  roasted pepper salad, 94
  Spanish omelette, 80
Pesto: tomato and pesto toasties, 31
Pizza: deep pan vegetable pizza, 53
  mushroom and pancetta pizzas, 56
  pepperoni pizza, 52
  tuna and prawn pizza, 54
  turkey and avocado pitta pizzas, 55
Plaice: fried fish goujons, 38
  Parmesan fish goujons, 47
Ploughman's pâté, 21
Popovers, mushroom popovers, 42
Pork and prawn toasts, 32
Potatoes: cheese and pepper potato
    skins, 68
  new potato and chive salad, 90
  potato skins with Cajun dip, 70

Spanish omelette, 80
  spicy baked potatoes, 74
  Tex-Mex baked potatoes with chilli, 79
  tuna fishcake bites, 43
Prawns: garlic chilli prawns, 38
  pork and prawn toasts, 32
  salmon and prawn fritters, 44
  tuna and prawn pizza, 54

Rice: lemon and herb risotto wedges, 78
  rice and cheese croquettes, 37

Salads: beetroot, chicory and orange
    salad, 94
  Caesar salad, 87
  chicken and taco salad, 88
  crisp fruity salad, 92
  lettuce and herb salad, 91
  Mexican mixed salad, 88
  new potato and chive salad, 90
  quick ratatouille salad, 92
  roasted pepper salad, 94
Salade Niçoise, 86
Salmon: salmon and prawn fritters, 44
  salmon filo parcels, 60
Samosas: curried lamb samosas, 58
  leek and Stilton samosas, 59
Sardines: wholemeal SLTs, 73
Smoked salmon: blinis with smoked
    salmon and dill cream, 23
  scrambled egg and salmon muffins, 80
Sole: fried fish goujons, 38
  Parmesan fish goujons, 47
Spanish omelette, 80
Spinach stuffed mushrooms, 41
Sweet potatoes: spiced sweet potato
    turnovers, 57
Sweetcorn: Mexican mixed salad, 88
  sweetcorn and bacon fritters, 36

Tacos: chicken and taco salad, 88
  tuna chilli tacos, 70
Tex-Mex baked potatoes with chilli, 79
Tomatoes: Mediterranean garlic toast, 32
  quick ratatouille salad, 92
  tomato and garlic muffin parcels,
  tomato and pesto toasties, 31
  tomato and cheese tarts, 60
  wholemeal SLTs, 73
Tuna: Salade Niçoise, 86
  tuna and prawn pizza, 54
  tuna chilli tacos, 70
  tuna croissants, 76
  tuna fishcake bites, 43
Turkey and avocado pitta pizzas, 55

Vegetables: deep pan vegetable pizza, 53
  pepper dips with crudités, 12
  quick ratatouille salad, 92
  raw vegetables with olive oil dip, 16
tangy avocado dip, 18

Walnuts: chicken, bacon and walnut
    terrine, 22
  nut and cheese stuffed celery sticks, 24
  nut patties with mango relish, 46
  stuffed devilled eggs, 24